Cultivating Competence

in

English

LEARNERS

Integrating Social-Emotional Learning
With Language and Literacy

MARGARITA ESPINO CALDERÓN
LISA TARTAGLIA

With HECTOR MONTENEGRO

Solution Tree | Press

a division of
Solution Tree

555 North Morton Street
Bloomington, IN 47404
800.733.6786 (toll free) / 812.336.7700
FAX: 812.336.7790

email: info@SolutionTree.com
SolutionTree.com

Visit go.SolutionTree.com/EL to download the free reproducibles in this book.

Printed in the United States of America

Library of Congress Cataloging-in-Publication Data

Names: Calderón, Margarita, author. | Tartaglia, Lisa, author.
Title: Cultivating competence in English learners : integrating
   social-emotional learning with language and literacy / Margarita Espino
   Calderón, Lisa Tartaglia.
Description: Bloomington, IN : Solution Tree Press, [2022] | Includes
   bibliographical references and index.
Identifiers: LCCN 2022022926 (print) | LCCN 2022022927 (ebook) | ISBN
   9781952812118 (Paperback) | ISBN 9781952812125 (eBook)
Subjects: LCSH: Affective education. | English language--Study and
   teaching--Foreign speakers. | Language arts--Correlation with content
   subjects. | Literacy--Study and teaching. | Interdisciplinary approach
   in education.
Classification: LCC LB1072 .C34 2022 (print) | LCC LB1072 (ebook) | DDC
   370.15/34--dc23/eng/20220926
LC record available at https://lccn.loc.gov/2022022926
LC ebook record available at https://lccn.loc.gov/2022022927

Solution Tree
Jeffrey C. Jones, CEO
Edmund M. Ackerman, President

Solution Tree Press
President and Publisher: Douglas M. Rife
Associate Publisher: Sarah Payne-Mills
Managing Production Editor: Kendra Slayton
Editorial Director: Todd Brakke
Art Director: Rian Anderson
Copy Chief: Jessi Finn
Production Editor: Gabriella Jones-Monserrate
Content Development Specialist: Amy Rubenstein
Acquisitions Editor: Sarah Jubar
Copy Editor: Mark Hain
Proofreader: Charlotte Jones
Text and Cover Designer: Fabiana Cochran
Associate Editor: Sarah Ludwig
Editorial Assistants: Charlotte Jones and Elijah Oates

Margarita would like to dedicate this book to her team of phenomenal educators and the amazing teachers and principals who have worked and are working with us.

Lisa would like to dedicate this book to her three children: Michala, Callie, and Anthony. They are the sun, moon, and stars in her life. She would also like to dedicate this book to all her amazing students. They continually encourage and challenge her to seek ways to make sure they are seen, heard, and valued.

Acknowledgments

We would like to acknowledge all the teachers, principals, and central district administrators from Loudoun, Virginia; Johnston County schools, North Carolina; Clint Integrated School District, Texas; Lindsay, California; and many other schools across the United States who have or are in the process of implementing the programs described here.

We are so grateful to Douglas Rife, Claudia Wheatley, and Jeff Jones for bringing continuous attention to and support for English learners. We thank our editor, Gabriella Jones-Monserrate, for her dedication to this publication.

Solution Tree Press would like to thank the following reviewers:

Jennifer Arias
  ELL and English Instructor
  Adlai Stevenson High School
  Lincolnshire, Illinois

Justin Fisk
  Director of World Languages and ELL
  Adlai Stevenson High School
  Lincolnshire, Illinois

Kimberly Freiley
  ELA Teacher
  Ingersoll Middle School
  Canton, Illinois

Susanna Lee
  Teacher
  Christopher High School
  Gilroy, California

Katie McCluskey
  Assistant Superintendent for Teaching,
    Learning, Accountability
  Glen Ellyn School District 41
  Glen Ellyn, Illinois

Katie Saunders
  Middle Level Teacher
  Anglophone School District West
  Woodstock, New Brunswick, Canada

Renae Skarin
  Curriculum Review Process Director
  English Learners Success Forum
  New York City, New York

Amy Swick
  Coordinator of EL/Bilingual
    Education
  Appleton Area School District
  Appleton, Wisconsin

Steven Weber
  Associate Superintendent for Teaching
    and Learning
  Fayetteville Public Schools
  Fayetteville, Arkansas

Visit **go.SolutionTree.com/EL** to download the free reproducibles in this book.

Table of Contents

Chapter 2
Self-Management Applied to Reading. 43

Chapter 3
Social Awareness Applied to Discourse. 77

Chapter 4
Responsible Decision Making Applied to Writing 99

Chapter 5

Relationship Skills Applied to School-Classroom Communities

About the Authors

Margarita Espino Calderón, PhD, is professor emerita and senior research scientist at the Johns Hopkins University School of Education. She has conducted research, training, and curriculum development for teaching language, reading comprehension, and content knowledge to K–12 English learners. Her work has focused on effective instructional processes, two-way and dual-language programs, teacher learning communities, and professional development for schools with minoritized-language populations and striving adolescent readers. Calderón's research has been supported by the Carnegie Corporation of New York, U.S. Department of Education, U.S. Department of Labor, National Institutes of Health, and the Texas Education Agency.

A native of Juárez, Mexico, Calderón is a recognized expert in education with more than one hundred publications to her credit. She is a respected member of several panels and national committees, and she has been welcomed internationally as a visiting lecturer. Calderón has created the *ExC-ELL*™ program and directed international institutes for administrators, teachers, and parents. She has experience as a classroom teacher, bilingual program director, professional development coordinator, professor of educational leadership graduate programs, and bilingual teacher supervisor.

Calderón earned a doctorate in multicultural education, applied linguistics, and organizational development through a joint doctorate program at Claremont Graduate University and San Diego State University.

Lisa Tartaglia is a high school assistant principal in Loudoun County Public Schools in Virginia. She has been an educator since 1994 with experiences as an elementary classroom teacher, reading specialist, and high school literacy coach. Tartaglia has taught in a variety of settings that range from working in a Title I, predominantly low-income school to a high-achieving school in an affluent area in Ashburn, Virginia. She was also an instructor for early childhood classes at the community college level and has presented at several conferences.

Tartaglia participated in the 2020–2021 Transformative Education Leadership cohort. She is also a consultant and trainer with Margarita Calderón and Associates. Tartaglia believes that all students can learn and advocates for equity in schools, especially focusing on literacy. She has helped create curriculum and culture changes for English learners in her school district.

Tartaglia received a bachelor's degree in elementary and early childhood education from East Stroudsburg University of Pennsylvania, a master's degree in reading from East Stroudsburg University, an endorsement in teaching English to speakers of other languages (TESOL) from The George Washington University in Washington, DC, and an endorsement in education leadership and supervision from Longwood University in Farmville, Virginia.

To book Margarita Espino Calderón or Lisa Tartaglia for professional development, contact pd@SolutionTree.com.

Introduction

Why Adapt Social-Emotional Learning For English Learners?

Most English learners spend only about thirty minutes a day in English as a second language (ESL) classes with an ESL teacher. In push-in classes, the time with ESL teachers may be as little as three minutes and the rest of the day spent with general education teachers. Given this reality, general education teachers need more efficient and effective ways to integrate social-emotional learning (SEL), language, and literacy development into all subjects and grade levels to have the most powerful learning impact, not just for English learners but for all students.

General education teachers find that an array of sheltered English strategies has not helped to create meaningful lessons, as evidenced by the multitude of English learners labeled *long-term English learners* who are unable to pass the language and literacy exit tests, don't reach grade-level status, and at times do not graduate from high school. *Sheltered English instruction* is a method of making academic instruction in English comprehensible for students with limited English proficiency. It is used in ESL and general education classrooms or specific, designated content classes (Parker, 1985). Teachers use visual aids, physical activities, and the environment to teach new words (Freeman & Freeman, 1988). Having to pick and choose the sequence of activities or which activity is better for writing than for reading lays a burden on the day-to-day decision making. Education scholars Jana Echevarría, MaryEllen Vogt, and Deborah J. Short (2008) developed a sheltered instruction observation protocol (SIOP) to provide a framework for developing lessons. However, as of February 2013, no studies within the scope of the English Language Learners review protocol had reviewed SIOP nor did it meet the design standards of What Works Clearinghouse (WWC, 2013). The WWC is a firm within the U.S. Department of Education that holds educational programs across the United States to high research standards to ensure programs, products, practices, and policies all operate effectively on the basis of scientific evidence (WWC, n.d.). Since it has not conducted any studies of SIOP, the WWC has not been able to draw any research-based conclusions as to whether SIOP effectively improves outcomes in lesson development (WWC, 2007).

Teachers want an evidence-based sequence of how, when, and where to integrate vocabulary. Now that social-emotional programs or competencies have become a major educational focus, that brings on an additional piece of a strange new instructional puzzle. Of course, we haven't even mentioned switching back and forth or simultaneously teaching in hybrid modes to a diverse group of students.

General education teachers in elementary schools and core content teachers in secondary schools can help English learners and all multilingual learners succeed in their classrooms with some instructional strategies for integrating vocabulary, discourse, reading comprehension, and writing in the content areas, all the while giving English learners strategies and the language to develop social-emotional skills and competencies.

English learners enrolled in bilingual or dual-language programs, or who learn as part of a schoolwide bilingual approach, have teachers who were most likely prepared to teach content in one or two languages. However, these students will also benefit from seeing the integration of language, literacy, core content, and SEL as presented in this book.

Social-Emotional Learning: Definition and Application

SEL, according to Committee for Children (2022), is "the process of developing self-awareness, self-control, interpersonal skills, and decision-making skills that are vital to school, work, and life success." Social-emotional learning during language and literacy instruction is a logical integration. When educators teach vocabulary, they can have students practice the SEL competencies of empathy, self-awareness, relationship building, or cooperation. Students can learn and apply other competencies as they read, discuss, and write in collaboration with peers.

Yet, SEL is not just about student competencies. The administration, teachers, coaches, cafeteria workers, and all other adults in a school need to practice their own SEL skills and dispositions as they shift from a deficit perception of English learners and multilingual learners to an assets-based acknowledgment of their personal, social, cultural, and linguistic strengths. When we take time to honor, acknowledge, and support students in feeling they are competent, we have a much better chance for supporting them to be successful in school and in their lives (Zacarian, Calderón, & Gottlieb, 2021).

There are several methodologies and lines of thinking about SEL competencies. The most well-known framework was developed by the Collaborative for Academic, Social, and Emotional Learning (CASEL, n.d.c), which defines *SEL* as follows:

> SEL is the process through which all young people and adults acquire and apply the knowledge, skills, and attitudes to develop healthy identities, manage emotions, achieve personal and collective goals, feel and show empathy for others, establish, and maintain supportive relationships, and make responsible and caring decisions.

The CASEL framework addresses five core competencies: (1) self-awareness, (2) self-management, (3) social awareness, (4) relationship skills, and (5) responsible decision making (CASEL, n.d.c).

SEL is intended to be implemented as a schoolwide culture. Figure I.1 (page 4) summarizes the CASEL (n.d.d) practices and policies in a comprehensive graphic.

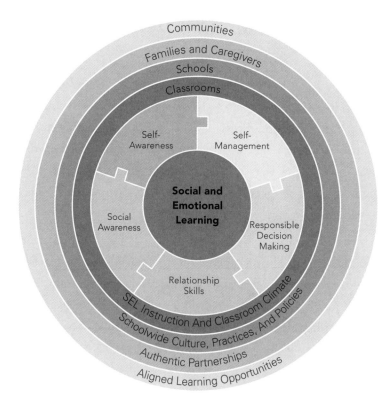

Source: © 2020 CASEL. Used with permission.

FIGURE I.1: The five CASEL SEL competencies.

This approach also easily aligns with the services a school can provide multilingual learners. Teachers at all grade levels and of any subject can teach and meet the social and emotional needs of English learners through practices and activities featured in each chapter. We build on the five CASEL competencies and their attributes by integrating them into strategies and lesson components that apply to English learners and multilingual learners but also work for all other students in the class. In this book, we share how you can practice and develop key SEL competencies not only during language or literacy learning but in all subject areas.

Goals of the CASEL Competencies

If SEL is to function systematically in the classroom, a schoolwide culture of SEL practices and policies must be established, as well as authentic partnerships with the multicultural learners and their families. Throughout the chapters in this book, we describe the aligned learning opportunities with the understanding that all instructional practices ought to support English learners and multilingual learners as part of the school's population, on school indicators like report cards, and with high principles for everyone.

The attributes of each SEL competency serve as a goal for students and adults to practice when they are working with others. It is in the context of interaction that one can become self-aware and aware of others, manage difficult situations, grow one's own dispositions and skills, build relationships, and make good decisions.

Different SEL Perspectives and Approaches

In addition to the methods we've already described, there are other approaches to addressing the core competencies. The RULER method was created by the Yale Center for Emotional Intelligence (YCEI) and is an acronym for the five skills of emotional intelligence: (1) recognizing, (2) understanding, (3) labeling, (4) expressing, and (5) regulating (YCEI, 2022). Their approach begins with the teachers and other education professionals, then addresses the students, and finally the families and communities (YCEI, 2022). Another program, Character Strong (characterstrong.com), focuses on the whole child with lessons and activities that incorporate the five SEL competencies.

SEL is not new, and educators have addressed it in various ways. Since 1978, the Johns Hopkins University models of cooperative learning have included what they call *social norms* for learning and interacting with others. Programs such as Success for All/Éxito Para Todos (SFA/EPT), Cooperative Integrated Reading and Composition (CIRC), Bilingual Cooperative Integrated Reading and Composition (BCIRC), and Expediting Comprehension for English Language Learners/ Acelerando la Comprensión en Español: Lectura, Escritura, y Razonamiento Académico (ExC-ELL/ACE-LERA) have all taught dispositions and behaviors for learning, self-regulation, tenacity, creativity, voice and choice, collaboration, diversity, and critical thinking, along with language processing, reading comprehension, and information-acquisition skills.

SFA/EPT and CIRC preK to sixth-grade reading and writing programs were developed by Robert Slavin and colleagues. The U.S. Department of Education's Institute for Education Sciences (USDOE IES) funded the research and development of these whole-school implementation programs that Slavin and colleagues designed to help all students develop reading and writing skills.

The BCIRC program for English learners in dual-language elementary schools and the ExC-ELL/ACE-LERA for grades 6–12, developed by Margarita Espino

Calderón and colleagues, were researched and developed specifically for English learners and for use in multilingual learner classrooms. Since the BCIRC program meets the Institute for Education Sciences criteria, the Carnegie Corporation of New York asked Calderón to conduct a five-year empirical study in several middle and high schools to train core content teachers on how to integrate language, reading comprehension, writing skills, and content in all classrooms.

In addition to the Johns Hopkins models, several prepackaged curricula and models have been created to focus on SEL. However, some of the ways in which educators have modeled and implemented SEL are now recognized as inequitable and, in some instances, harmful to children of color, as research by the National Equity Project (n.d.) indicates. Some models use a deficit mindset and focus on classroom discipline. They force students to self-regulate or self-manage when they may not yet have attained the skills to do these things, and some seek disciplinary measures when students are noncompliant (National Equity Project, n.d.).

CASEL (n.d.c) addresses these issues of inequity as follows:

> SEL advances educational equity and excellence through authentic school-family-community partnerships to establish learning environments and experiences that feature trusting and collaborative relationships, rigorous and meaningful curriculum and instruction, and ongoing evaluation. SEL can help address various forms of inequity and empower young people and adults to co-create thriving schools and contribute to safe, healthy, and just communities.

Educators must view addressing the social-emotional needs of English learners through a lens of equity and academic achievement. Some recently arrived English learners or newcomers come with trauma, fears, and intense emotional issues due to their war-torn country, experiences with extortion, and so on. On their way to this country, they may have suffered violence and even loss of family members. Some come with cultural beliefs that do not align with the five competencies, such as finding value in showing assertiveness, differing ways of showing respect, and ways of solving conflict. Therefore, educators must explicitly teach those competencies to adults in a school and to newcomers to help them feel supported in their new learning environment.

Academically, English learners show overall declines, particularly in speaking (Najarro, 2021). Without digital equity, many English learners, like many other students, did not have access to remote learning during the pandemic and missed out on quality instruction. Moreover, some may have suffered the loss of family members due to COVID or deportation. Not attending school had a more detrimental effect on the younger English learners. They missed out on learning sufficient vocabulary, mathematics, learning how to learn, and basic interaction skills. Now, there is danger of elementary schools sending more long-term English learners to middle schools, and then on to high schools. In my estimation, the majority of English learners across the United States are long-term English learners. They are students who have been in U.S. schools since kindergarten or for more than six years and are still learning English in secondary schools because they haven't passed the exit exams. Data from Regional Educational Laboratory West (REL West) indicate that the percentage of long-term English learners in New York City, Chicago, Colorado, and California ranged from 23 percent to 74 percent in 2013–2014, and that the number in California grew from 344,862 in 2008 to 380,995 in 2015 and continues to increase (REL West, 2016). Middle and high school English learners and multilingual learners need to develop self-awareness, self-motivation, and self-management to catch up with what they missed and to catch up with their peers. They need the skills to develop the type of self-esteem, fortitude, and relationships that will boost their confidence in learning.

The five CASEL SEL competencies can best be taught in the context of learning to speak, listen, understand, read, and write in English. We find that the intentional teaching of language and literacy in all areas of the curriculum can support the social-emotional needs of all students. Further, there are SEL competencies that align quite nicely with all instructional strategies and learning activities.

There will be times when recommendations for instruction in this book for general education teachers are more applicable to a specific cohort of students, such as recent arrivals. Otherwise, they will be applicable to all multilingual learners, English learners, and other students in general education classrooms.

Who English Learners Are

In this book, we use the terms *multilingual learners* as inclusive of all current and former *English learners*, as well as any learner who speaks another language or has a different home culture. A teacher might have a roomful of multilingual learners from different cultures who speak different languages. Some may be English learners, and some might not.

Those of non-English learner status include the following (Gottlieb, 2022; Gottlieb & Calderón, 2023).	Those who are English learners include the following (Gottlieb, 2022).
• Reclassified or exited students • Dual-language program learners from English-speaking backgrounds • Those never identified as English learners but who are from linguistically and culturally diverse backgrounds • Heritage learners	• Newcomers and recently arrived English learners • Highly schooled newcomers • Students with limited or interrupted formal education • Dually identified special education and English learners • Long-term English learners • Gifted and talented students

In some cases, these students were called *sheltered English learners*, but that is not an official category. In fact, many regard the term as condescending. Not all students have been in sheltered classrooms. Besides, sheltered instruction, as mentioned by the Institute of Education Sciences' WWC (2013), is not an effective instructional model and has not helped long-term English learners. Long-term English learners probably did not receive adequate or quality instruction on academic English, reading, and writing. Perhaps they were "sheltered" too much and were given watered-down curriculum. Perhaps their teachers' low expectations did not include rigorous instruction that addressed their individual needs. Organizations such as the Carnegie Corporation of New York began to bring panels of researchers together to find existing research on addressing long-term English learners' needs (Short & Fitzsimmons, 2007). Since no valid studies were found, they funded a study of BCIRC in grades 6 to 12 that was later called ExC-ELL.

Who This Book Is For

After studying and observing the implementation of ExC-ELL in hundreds of classrooms, we realized that the best student outcomes were coming from schools that implemented the program schoolwide. This is the premise behind the instructional and professional development model. A schoolwide program includes all educators, students, and families in the schools.

Therefore, this book is written for:

- General education teachers in K–12 schools
- Instructional coaches for all subjects
- ESL or English development (ELD) teachers
- ESL administrators and resource specialists
- Bilingual or dual-language teachers
- Bilingual or dual-language administrators and resource specialists

Home-to-school and family outreach coordinators, social workers, counselors, administrators, coaches, and families can also benefit from content in this book, as some strategies and content directly apply to them. Educators can use the instructional strategies in the book to offer workshops for parents and caregivers.

Base of Research for This Book

The ExC-ELL components mentioned in this book were tested in dozens of schools in various states to compare outcomes for students with students in other programs. In addition to English learners in ExC-ELL making significant academic and language growth, the non-English learners in the same classrooms also achieved more in language, literacy, and subject matter. In fact, the experimental middle and high schools implementing ExC-ELL went from low performing to exemplary in two years.

The control schools had the typical sheltered instruction models or popular ways of teaching vocabulary, reading, and writing. The experimental schools had the ExC-ELL model constructed from solid research by national language and literacy panels (August & Shanahan, 2006, 2008; National Literacy Panel, 2000). Once the model was constructed, it was tested in classrooms by general education teachers of mathematics, science, social studies, and language arts. English learners in these experimental schools outperformed those in control schools in the Woodcock-Muñoz Vocabulary and Reading Batteries and district indicators such as state exams and graduation rates. The ExC-ELL model continues to be implemented by Margarita Calderón and Associates in hundreds of classrooms across the United States and shows exemplary results.

In addition to the English approach, a bilingual or dual-language model for elementary schools was also developed for English and Spanish instruction. This model was also tested using matched experimental and control schools. Its description and significant results in English and Spanish for the experimental group are found in the WWC (n.d.). The majority of English learners in BCIRC were able to exit from English learner status at third grade and the rest at fourth grade. Most important, those students saw their Spanish proficiency and appreciation of their home language grow at significant levels. Thus, all the instructional strategies in this book can be taught in two languages. In fact, using the same methodologies and routines makes it easier and safer for students to accelerate their learning.

All students in BCIRC and ExC-ELL of different language proficiencies in their first and second languages were able to develop listening, speaking, reading, and writing in both languages at higher levels when vocabulary, reading, and writing were learned through ample peer interaction in pairs, triads, and quads (Calderón, 2007b, 2012; Calderón, Hertz-Lazarowitz, & Slavin, 1998; Calderón & Minaya-Rowe, 2011). Working with peers gave students opportunities to put into practice SEL competencies and accelerate their language and literacy development, as you will see in this book.

Interaction is the key to learning for English learners. As illustrated in figure I.2 (page 11), vocabulary and language patterns are the key to meaningful quality interaction and information processing in any language (CASEL, 2021). As we will show in the upcoming chapters, SEL is at the center of all teaching and learning and leverages the home culture and language.

Vocabulary and discourse are the foundation for reading and writing. Both value and affirm the students' use of languages for learning while they strive to become bilingual and biliterate.

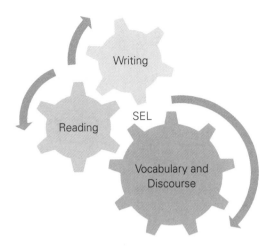

FIGURE I.2: Integration of vocabulary, reading, writing, and SEL.

How to Use This Book

The five broad, interrelated areas of competence CASEL (n.d.d) identifies—(1) self-awareness, (2) self-management, (3) social awareness, (4) relationship skills, and (5) responsible decision making—also apply to the relationship between educators and families. They offer potential solutions to the school priorities of academics, equity, mental health, civic learning, and college and career readiness. Across this book's five chapters, we look at these priorities from a multilingual learner's frame of reference.

Each chapter defines and focuses on applying one of the five competencies in the classroom for English learners. However, the competencies can be taught across all instructional events. Chapters begin with a vignette that tells about an English learner, defines the competency, and provides activities or practices teachers can use in the classroom to incorporate the competency. Each chapter also offers other practical information to support English learners, see their strengths and assets, teach how to work collaboratively, problem solve, and provide English learners opportunities to express their unique gifts. Throughout the chapters, you will see guidance for the design of a lesson and the instructional strategies to use, ways students can apply competencies, and the feedback that will anchor competencies.

The chapters break down as follows.

- **Chapter 1, "Self-Awareness Applied to Vocabulary and Discourse":** All students need academic vocabulary instruction to master content areas and SEL competencies. This chapter introduces and provides directions for the seven-step method for preteaching vocabulary, as well as research on academic vocabulary, knowledge about how SEL can be part of vocabulary instruction, discourse about the impact of SEL on vocabulary, and tools for educators and families.

- **Chapter 2, "Self-Management Applied to Reading":** This chapter presents a systematic way to teach reading in the content areas. We integrate decoding, comprehension, vocabulary learning, and discourse for English learners. We share a comprehensive approach and basic steps for teaching the five reading components recommended by the National Reading Panel and the National Literacy Panel for Language Minority Children and Youth.

- **Chapter 3, "Social Awareness Applied to Discourse":** This chapter describes various cooperative learning activities that encourage discourse as well as self and teamwork reflection. English learners need opportunities to talk with other students. They need to be able to discuss what they are learning. Classrooms that provide cooperative learning and teamwork are safe places for students to talk. Engaging in discourse supports SEL in all content areas.

- **Chapter 4, "Responsible Decision Making Applied to Writing":** SEL undergirds writing, which is both social and emotional. Writing in the primary language helps multilingual learners express their profound feelings and can be therapeutic. This chapter shows how writing based on a mentor text helps students become more proficient writers. We describe tools for editing and revising, and strategies for creative writing.

- **Chapter 5, "Relationship Skills Applied to School-Classroom Communities":** Schools need to be intentional about building trust with students and families. Teachers need support as well. This chapter dives into establishing safe learning environments both in physical and virtual classrooms and provides ways schools can create opportunities to mend previous inequities.

We include a brief fact sheet in the introduction of every chapter called The Research On . . . . These fact sheets list foundational and current research about the skills explored in the corresponding chapter and summarize the importance of applying the accompanying SEL competency to them.

Each chapter also features other recurring content sections.

- We explore SEL across all content areas in middle and high schools through a section applying the chapter's respective SEL competency to all curriculum content areas. We also provide research and strategies for integrating the competency into lessons.

- We adapt the strategies, research, and content in the chapter for elementary-grade students.

- At the end of each chapter, in a feature called Questions From the Field, we address frequently asked questions about the chapter's respective SEL competency and curriculum and supply actionable answers.

The shift schools are increasingly making after the events of the COVID-19 pandemic offers an opportunity for educators to discard ineffective past practices and instead implement those that work for multilingual learners and their peers. In particular, this book's final chapter brings language, literacy, SEL, and core content together under the rubric of relationship skills and teacher learning communities. We include practices and protocols that will help plan effective professional learning, coaching, and follow-up support systems for accelerating English learners' and multilingual learners' academic growth and well-being.

Self-Awareness Applied to Vocabulary and Discourse

Joanna, a high school English learner, came to class eager to learn every day. She was doing well in her English learner (EL) classes and learning more English each day. One day, Joanna's EL teacher learned that she was skipping one of her classes. The EL teacher checked, and while Joanna was in attendance for school, she was not going to her biology class. The teacher approached Joanna one morning and asked her about biology class. Joanna looked at the ground and did not respond. The teacher asked her again, and then Joanna started to cry. This was not like her, so the EL teacher asked her what was wrong. Joanna told her she did not want to go to biology class because she said it was too hard. The EL teacher was surprised because science was Joanna's favorite subject.

The EL teacher decided to go to the next biology class to see why it was so hard for Joanna. While observing the class, the EL teacher noticed that, for most of the class, the students sat and took notes while the teacher lectured. Then, the students would answer questions about the notes and perform a lab that coincided with the lecture. There was no time during the lecture for students to talk about what they learned, vocabulary was not pretaught, and students were not reading or writing about the text. She saw Joanna trying to take notes, and when it came time to do the lab, Joanna stayed in her seat and put her head down. The teacher went over to her, gave her a different paper, and said something, but Joanna kept her head down.

The biology teacher approached the EL teacher and said that she did not know what to do to help Joanna. The teacher thought the class was too hard for Joanna and that she didn't know the concepts, so she gave Joanna an alternative assignment she thought would be less confusing than participating in the lab activity. As a result, Joanna did not participate in the lab; she just kept her head down.

Joanna was very interested in biology. She wanted to learn the concepts, even if they were difficult. However, she needed some support to access the curriculum. Joanna's teacher could pre-teach the vocabulary and provide sentence frames or stems to help engage in conversations about the concepts. Instead of providing her with an alternative assignment, the teacher could keep the rigor and provide scaffolds to help Joanna learn the content. Giving her that support would help her to feel more comfortable and engaged.

SEL and Academic Language

In this chapter, we examine the SEL competency of self-awareness and how it can be developed while teaching and learning academic language, starting with the smallest denominator: vocabulary.

Teachers will learn the following three items.

1. Why it is important to teach vocabulary, academic language, and oral discourse

2. What it takes to effectively integrate self-awareness development into vocabulary instruction

3. How to teach vocabulary and academic language to English learners, multilingual learners, and all students whose comprehension of academic language might have been impacted by the COVID-19 hiatus

Students will have the following four tools.

1. A rich corpus of different vocabulary that cuts across all subject areas

2. Strategies for learning more words

3. Strategies for becoming self-aware

4. Words and phrases to express their feelings, concerns, and needs

Teaching vocabulary is the first step in developing effective reading and writing skills with English learners. Aside from these skills, English learners cannot effectively acquire the academic language of any subject area without the integration of the social-emotional side of learning. English learners will often appear shy and might be reluctant to speak. They might be afraid of being ridiculed and embarrassed. If teachers know, understand, and integrate the core SEL competencies into the instructional framework, it will be easier to create safe spaces for learning so that English learners can do the following.

- Become motivated and inspired to actively participate in the learning process

- Feel safe to make mistakes

- Have tools to communicate with the teachers and peers

Students gain self-awareness of their reluctance to speak English as they go through the seven ExC-ELL vocabulary steps for learning a word or phrase. Later in this chapter, we discuss how step 6 helps English learners and their peers become aware of their dispositions, tenacity, and strength.

Personalizing the core SEL competencies means that adults reflect deeply on how the structure of the classroom space and the delivery of a lesson facilitate inclusion and how the context will encourage respect, caring, safety, and empathy in the learning community during vocabulary and language instruction in all subject areas. These competencies are also key for the non-English learners who partner with English learners for vocabulary learning because they need to practice empathy, caring, patience, and respect toward the English learners. For all students, self-awareness is crucial to learning academic language, down to the basics of vocabulary. From that foundation, we discuss the intersection of vocabulary and discourse and provide strategies for increasing self-awareness in discourse. To conclude the chapter, we explore vocabulary, discourse, and self-awareness instruction in the elementary grades and for administrators, coaches, family, and caregivers.

Vocabulary: The Foundation of Academic Language

Researchers, such as those featured in the upcoming section titled The Research on Vocabulary and Academic Language (page 19), have been telling us to be more explicit about teaching the vocabulary of mathematics, science, social studies, and English language arts, as doing so helps students succeed in those subjects. This is academic English. Teaching vocabulary or academic English is not just for English language teachers. Every teacher in every school needs to be a vocabulary and language teacher. English learners, including refugees and other newcomers, especially benefit from schools that adopt this mindset. After the disruption to learning in the wake of the COVID-19 pandemic, every teacher is also an SEL, vocabulary, and language teacher since most students will have experienced limited or interrupted formal education and lag behind due to lack of academic language practice.

Vocabulary methods are often either too fluffy (superficial), too lengthy, or too unengaging to be effective. They are fluffy in the sense that the learning doesn't take hold, and teachers feel the need to reteach these words the next day. They are too unengaging when it's mostly dictionary work or copying definitions from the whiteboard into worksheets. Silent activities such as drawing pictures to represent meaning do not hold students accountable for producing these words verbally in meaningful contexts and do not anchor them in their brains and in their active verbal repertoires.

These methods keep students busy but take up too much precious time away from reading, where students learn more language.

In our experience, vocabulary classroom activities that are silent, such as worksheets, are particularly disliked among long-term English learners. As the chapter-opening scenario illustrates, long-term English learners have spent most of their school years doing worksheets and other low-level tasks while their peers participated in more creative and challenging endeavors.

Finding a balance between exciting but rigorous learning is what this book is all about. SEL strategies will undergird the balance between rigor and excitement that will motivate students to want to learn vocabulary, become curious about depth of word knowledge, and feel comfortable practicing with peers.

The challenge for teachers is to plan which words to teach, structure student talk and practice routines, set norms of interaction, and construct safe spaces in every lesson for integrating vocabulary instruction. Safe spaces with scaffolds are necessary for English learners to participate and contribute to class discussions. However, in a year or two it will be necessary to gradually remove the scaffolds—but never the safe space. We will take you through these steps and share which scaffolds work and do not take up so much time.

The Research on Vocabulary and Academic Language

Several studies detailed in this feature provide insight into the impact of vocabulary study on student reading comprehension, word acquisition, and overall performance in class. The following shows just how important it is to begin teaching vocabulary words in lessons as early in a student's education as possible. Much of the research, as you will see, has been around for many years, yet it has not trickled down into curriculum and instructional practices.

- Vocabulary in kindergarten and first grade is a significant predictor of reading comprehension or reading difficulties in the middle and secondary grades (August & Shanahan, 2006; Chall, 1996; Cunningham & Stanovich, 1998; National Reading Panel, 2000).

- The average six-year-old has a vocabulary of approximately eight thousand words and learns three to five thousand more per year (Sénéchal & Cornell, 1993).

- By the end of twelfth grade, students should have learned fifty thousand words (Graves & Sales, 2013).

- Command of a large vocabulary frequently sets high-achieving English learners and multilingual learners apart from less successful ones (Calderón, 2007b; Calderón & Slakk, 2017).

- The number of words heard in an hour at home by children of poverty is about 615; by middle-class children, about 1,251; and by children of professionals, about 2,153 (Hart & Risley, 1995).

- Vocabulary knowledge is knowledge of how the word fits into the world (Stahl, 2005).

- Active participation by students during teacher read-alouds contributes to vocabulary growth. For example, open-ended questions, function-attribute questions (as opposed to pointing without speaking), and multiple exposures to words during shared reading facilitate students' production of those words (Calderón, Trower, Tartaglia, & Montenegro, 2022).

- Teaching vocabulary helps develop phonological awareness (Nagy, 2005) and reading comprehension (Beck & McKeown, 1991).

- Vocabulary instruction needs to be explicitly taught before, during, and after reading to help English learners catch up with the words they are missing (Calderón, 2007b, 2022; Calderón et al., 2005; Calderón & Minaya-Rowe, 2003; Calderón & Slakk, 2017).

- Vocabulary instruction needs to be long term and comprehensive (Nagy, 2005) for English learners (Calderón et al., 2005; Carlo, August, & Snow, 2005).

- English learners need discussions about word knowledge, including cognates, affixes, pronunciation, decoding, multiple meanings, phrasal clusters, and idioms, using the word in question (Calderón, 2007b).

Most English learners miss out on explicit instruction of vocabulary and academic discourse. In our five-year studies on teaching English learners in high schools, we found ways that students can attain disciplinary knowledge through the following integrated sequence of explicit instruction in language, literacy, and the core content areas.

- Vocabulary → reading → vocabulary → writing → metacognitive skills → SEL competencies = content knowledge
- Talk it → Do it → Talk it → Read it → Talk it → Write it

Please see the introduction (page 1) for more information about our studies. Other components of the sequence are further explained in each chapter.

The more words English learners and multilingual learners know, the faster they learn to speak, listen, discuss, read, and write. Researchers have told us for quite some time that the vocabulary students know and are reading by the end of first grade predicts how well they perform in middle and high school (Chall, 1986). The myth that it takes seven to ten years to learn a language has done "irreparable harm" as EL education expert Laurie Olsen (2010), titles her publication because it creates a mindset of *I don't have to worry about them this year; they have time to learn*. These low expectations and lack of academic rigor are examples of the irreparable harm that needs dramatic changes in mindsets and school policies.

With this in mind, in our experience working with educators, we have developed ways of changing mindsets for teachers, coaches, administrators, and students through integrated approaches that show almost immediate results and serve to motivate students and teachers. We will now focus on the integration of SEL with vocabulary mastery and discourse development through structured talk routines for the purpose of establishing the base for reading comprehension, academic writing, and learning content in the process.

Discourse Support for Self-Awareness in All Content Areas

Discourse is formal and orderly discussion, usually an extended expression of thought on a subject, connected with speech, writing, or a linguistic unit (such as a conversation or a story) larger than a sentence. Discourse is a mode of organizing knowledge, ideas, or experience that is rooted in language and its concrete contexts. In other words, science, social studies, language arts, mathematics, and other disciplines have their own discourse, and so does ESL. The language for processing an algebra problem is very different from discussing historical events in social studies. Therefore, to go beyond ESL-type discourse, all core content teachers want their students to learn the vocabulary and the discourse of their subject.

Self-awareness vocabulary is explicitly taught so that English learners can express how they feel and what they desire. A study by education scholar Lourdes Santiago-Poventud and colleagues (2015) analyzes the SELF program, in which students read books and learned SEL vocabulary two to three times a week. The researchers found that participating students showed growth with their ability to use SEL words in context. This empowered them to be able to discuss their feelings and led to improvement socially and academically. Table 1.1 shows a list of the kinds of words students learn in general SEL education that could help English learners express their emotions during their English acquisition.

TABLE 1.1: SEL Words for English Learners

Anger	Upset	Frustrated	Ability
Efficacy	Goals	Expectations	Embarrassed
Responsible	Consequences	Cooperated	Nervous
Challenge	Pleased	Emotions	Strength
Weakness	Achieve	Success	Confused
Mad	Excited	Tired	Annoyed
Scared	Growth	Mindset	Anxious

These or similar words could also be taught in the student's home language. Some students might not have the right words to express what is bothering them, even in their home language. A family liaison or school nurse can have a list handy to assist.

It is imperative for English learners to acquire the language to express their needs, hurts, and feelings beyond academic content. In addition to vocabulary, English learners will need discourse structures, such as sentence starters or sentence frames.

Newcomers and English learners will need simple phrases and prompts such as the following.

- "I feel _____."
- "I want _____."
- "I need _____."
- "May I _____?"
- "How do I _____?"
- "What is _____?"

English learners at higher proficiency levels will benefit from learning to listen to and use specificity in their discussions as they learn more sophisticated words and phrases, such as those listed in figure 1.1. Teachers can post SEL vocabulary in their classrooms in creative ways, such as the word tree pictured on this page.

honesty
commitment
reactions
kindness
empathy
respect feelings
patience action
tenacity
persistence
selflessness
humility
forgiveness
mindfulness
resilience

FIGURE 1.1: Word tree.

This type of mindful growth in vocabulary and depth of knowledge of self allows students to express their feelings and desires more precisely and to better understand emotions and the contexts in which they occur.

Strategies for Increasing Self-Awareness in Discourse and Vocabulary Acquisition

Vocabulary acquisition precedes all the following strategies. To teach the academic language of science, technology, engineering, art, and mathematics (STEAM), to say nothing of English language arts, social studies, physical education, music, and other subjects, teachers can prepare ahead of time by selecting words to teach and deciding which to teach at the beginning of a lesson and which to teach later in the lesson. Teachers can analyze the text they will use to select words English learners are most likely to need before they read for comprehension. Therefore, before teaching vocabulary, teachers need to learn the types and categories of words to make better selections for which words to teach. Table 1.2 samples words from tier 1; these are simple, everyday words that most students know by second grade, but English learners may not necessarily know.

TABLE 1.2: Tier 1 Words and Phrases

Afraid	Frustrated	Sorry
Apologize	Headache	Stomachache
Draw	Imagine	Stubborn
Draw a conclusion	In danger	Weigh
Drawer	Nausea	Weight
Excited	Shy	Write down

*Visit **go.SolutionTree.com/EL** for a free reproducible version of this table.*

Tier 2 words are information-processing words, such as connectors or sophisticated, polysemous words. Many tier 2 words are useful to express SEL needs, goals, and processing of the five competencies. See how many SEL utility words you can find in table 1.3, showing tier 2 words, and underline them.

TABLE 1.3: Tier 2 Words and Phrases

Absence	Contrast	Impact
Accordingly	Contributes to	Impact
Accuracy	Core	Implicit

Additive	Criteria	Increase
Affect	Criticize	Initially
Allow	Crucial	Interpret
Analogous	Define	Known as
Analyze	Denote	Notwithstanding
Apparent	Depict	Oddly
Approach	Describe	Predict
Arrange	Designate	Primarily due to
Articulate	Despite	Reason
As stated in	Detail	Reduce
Ask	Develop	Remark
Assortment	Device	Report
Assumption	Diagram	So that
Base	Discuss	Solely
Basis	Display	State
Behavior	Distinct	Straight chain
Belief	Distinguish	Subsequently
Body	Due to	Successive
Boundary	Effect	Suggest
Build	Emphasize	Summarize
Causes	Enumerate	To graph
Clarify	Explain	To map
Classify	Express	To plot
Coincide	Forthcoming	To state
Comment	Generate	Truncated
Communicate	Have been noted as	Trunk
Communicate	Hypothesize	Underlying
Compare	Identify	Vary
Compiled	Illustrate	Whereby
Conclude	Illustrate	Widespread
Concur	Organize	
Deplete	Perform	

*Visit **go.SolutionTree.com/EL** for a free reproducible version of this table.*

Our recommendation is that you select mainly tier 2 words to preteach in the content areas. ESL, ELD, or bilingual teachers can teach tier 1 words, along with other, lesson-related tier 2 and 3 words.

These words come from the mentor text the students are about to read and use as a model for their writing. We recommend selecting five words to preteach at the beginning of a lesson. These are key words that help students comprehend the tier 3 words (subject-specific words such as *photosynthesis*) that are usually found in the glossary. Most ESL and English language arts programs highlight the words to teach. Yet, you'll find that these are usually unfamiliar words such as *parka* that students might not use again beyond the text they are reading. In other words, they are not the most advantageous for English learners.

The words and phrases that have high utilitarian value (such as *accordingly, contrast, underlying,* and *forthcoming*) are tier 2 words because students can use them across all subject areas. Unless students understand those tier 2 words or phrases, it will be very difficult to grasp the concept of tier 3 words such as *photosynthesis, metaphor, simile,* or mathematical terminology. Tier 3 words are subject-specific words, often called academic or technical words. Table 1.4 samples tier 3 words and phrases.

TABLE 1.4: Tier 3 Words and Phrases

Atmospheric	Species	Habitat
Carbon structure	Electrons	Heat-trapping gases
Cretaceous	Extinction	Osmosis
Ecosystem shift	Habitable zone	Photosynthesis

*Visit **go.SolutionTree.com/EL** for a free reproducible version of this table.*

Note that SEL competency words—*self-awareness, self-management, social awareness, relationship, decision making, mindfulness,* and *empathy*—are also tier 3 words.

Selecting five high-utility words and phrases serves as scaffolding to help students enter the text with more confidence and understand a little better. Of course, as they read with a partner, they can learn more words. See chapter 2 (page 42) on reading for the description of this process and the huge role that vocabulary and verbal discourse plays in developing reading comprehension.

Preteach Five Words at the Beginning of Each Class Using the Seven-Step Method

After analyzing the text you will assign students to read, select five words, mainly from tier 2 and some from tier 3. Preteaching words doesn't just occur before reading a text. You should also teach key vocabulary before lesson explanations, videos, lab experiments, research projects, and other academic endeavors. Mention other words English learners might find unfamiliar during your explanations.

We have tested and compared a specific seven-step method for preteaching vocabulary with other vocabulary teaching methods (Calderón, 2011). We prefer the seven steps over other methods because five words can be taught in ten minutes, whereas other methods take up to twenty minutes to teach one word. The benefits of preteaching a word or phrase in two minutes not only saves time but also develops an in-depth understanding through verbal interaction with that word as students use it with a peer for a whole minute. The teacher can ask two pairs to share their examples. Figure 1.2 details the seven-step method for preteaching vocabulary.

1 The teacher says the word and asks students to repeat the word three times.

2 The teacher provides the context for the word using the actual sentence that students will read.

3 The teacher provides the dictionary definition of the word or phrase; this helps English learners begin to understand academic language.

4 The teacher explains the word or phrase with simple and understandable terms for the students.

5 The teacher highlights one characteristic of the word: grammar, spelling, polysemy, or cognate, for example.

6 The teacher provides a sentence frame or starter using the target word for students to use in oral practice with a partner; student pairs should produce about twelve examples in complete sentences.

7 The teacher informs students that they must learn the word or phrase because they will see it in their reading and will be expected to use it in peer reading, verbal summaries, exit slips (short, written responses to teacher-provided prompts at the end of class), and so on.

FIGURE 1.2: Seven-step method for preteaching vocabulary.

*Visit **go.SolutionTree.com/EL** for a free reproducible version of this figure.*

Figure 1.3 shows a sample application of the seven-step method for preteaching vocabulary.

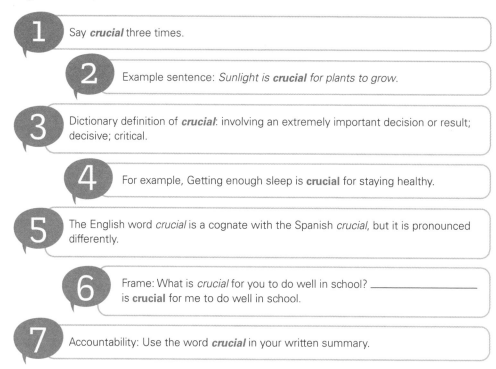

1 — Say *crucial* three times.

2 — Example sentence: *Sunlight is **crucial** for plants to grow.*

3 — Dictionary definition of ***crucial***: involving an extremely important decision or result; decisive; critical.

4 — For example, Getting enough sleep is **crucial** for staying healthy.

5 — The English word *crucial* is a cognate with the Spanish *crucial*, but it is pronounced differently.

6 — Frame: What is *crucial* for you to do well in school? _____ is **crucial** for me to do well in school.

7 — Accountability: Use the word ***crucial*** in your written summary.

FIGURE 1.3: Example of using the seven-step method.

There is a multitude of SEL and academic growth opportunities for English learners when using the seven-step method in all subject areas daily. Step 1 allows students to practice pronunciation collectively at least three times per word. For English learners who have been traumatized by negative classroom experiences, step 1 makes it safer for them to attempt pronunciation without the fear of being ridiculed and embarrassed because the entire class must pronounce the word together several times. This gradual rebuilding of self-confidence helps multilingual learners and especially English learners overcome that mythical silent period (Lomba, 2012) and the pain of suffering in silence and alone. The *silent period* is an untested hypothesis we use to explain delays in language development.

Step 1 provides English learners an excellent opportunity to be more reflective of their own fears and to take steps to overcome them while feeling greater empathy toward other English learners who may be experiencing the same debilitating negative self-perception and fixed mindset about their abilities. The simplicity of step 1 is deceiving. It is multisensory, phonetically engaging, and a fun activity, meeting the criteria of three of the five SEL competencies: (1) self-awareness, (2) self-management, and (3) social awareness.

Steps 2 through 5 are highly instructive and allow the teacher to succinctly explain the target word in a variety of ways to help the student hear the word in both a formal and a friendly definition and learn a characteristic of the word. This enables comprehension of the meaning, which gives students more self-assurance when using the word in their own examples in the next step.

Step 6 provides the greatest impact on cognitive, social, and emotional skills. This is when students work in pairs to orally practice and produce complete sentences based on the prompt given by the teacher. It is important that the pairing of students for step 6 be done prior to initiating the seven-step method. There are multiple ways of pairing students for this step for the purpose of developing social-emotional skills to support their academic achievement and English language proficiency. Therefore, do not leave the pairing process to chance. Make every effort to pair English learners with stronger English speakers. (Allowing students to self-select a partner tends to exclude timid or shy students.) Later, when English learners are comfortable in the classroom, you can expand methods for selecting partners. Use techniques such as academic vocabulary buddies to help students make new friends in a safe social learning environment and develop an appreciation for other cultures. Academic vocabulary buddies is a way to randomly pair students. The teacher distributes tier 2 words on cards. There are two of each. The students find their academic buddy and sit together for that lesson.

For instance, in step 6, some of the prompts can be a sentence starter or a sentence frame, such as the previous example, _____ *is crucial for me to do well in school.* The blank can be in any part of a sentence; for example, *It is crucial that I _____ so that I can do well in school.* Step 6 must be carefully crafted so that it generates five or six examples from each partner. Test the frames in your head before you give them to students.

The power of this step is that even newcomers can start practicing English from day one, and even if they don't know a word of English, they can mimic what their partner is saying. This creates a safe learning environment for newcomers to participate and motivates them to want to experiment with language with a partner (whom they might not have had an opportunity to make friends with) in a traditional classroom environment. Using the words in context also affords students the opportunity to further practice social conventions. This repeated oral practice further enhances listening, communication, and cooperation skills. Overall, step 6 gives

English learners the opportunity to establish and maintain healthy and rewarding relationships, further strengthening relationship-skill competencies.

Step 7 places additional value and importance on the words and holds students accountable for knowing and using the words multiple times in exit slips, oral discourse, reading, and writing. Figure 1.4 shows an example of defining and learning a new SEL term.

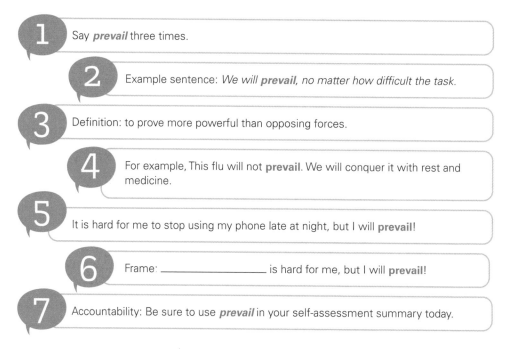

1 Say *prevail* three times.

2 Example sentence: *We will **prevail**, no matter how difficult the task.*

3 Definition: to prove more powerful than opposing forces.

4 For example, This flu will not **prevail**. We will conquer it with rest and medicine.

5 It is hard for me to stop using my phone late at night, but I will **prevail**!

6 Frame: _____ is hard for me, but I will **prevail**!

7 Accountability: Be sure to use *prevail* in your self-assessment summary today.

FIGURE 1.4: Example of using the seven-step method to teach SEL language.

This practice of preteaching vocabulary helps students contextualize language at multiple dimensions rather than looking up words in the dictionary and filling out boring worksheets. The result is that English learners are more empowered to make healthy decisions regarding their short-term academic goals as well as begin to consider their long-term career goals.

Use the seven-step method for explicit instruction of vocabulary not just for teaching self-awareness but all SEL vocabulary. Teaching words such as *happiness, appreciation, empathy, gratitude, diversity, efficacy, restorative practices, fixed mindset,* and *growth mindset* strengthens students' ability to be self-aware of their responsibility for learning words every day. These can also help them better label and more effectively manage their emotions.

Use Table Tents

Table tents are folded cards that display new vocabulary terms used in a lesson. You can use table tents as tools for learning like flash cards or as visual reminders of the vocabulary students are meant to learn. Asynchronous table tents can be printed and laminated. Synchronous table tents can live in Google Docs or Padlets or any useful place readily accessible to students. The table tents can also contain the SEL language that English learners need for working in pairs or teams. These include tier 2 words and phrases and key tier 3 words. Some table tents can also contain checklists for self-assessment, as you can see in figure 1.5, which shows an example of a table tent.

Self-Awareness and Self-Assessment

☐ Growth mindset

☐ Efficient

☐ Empathetic

☐ Happy

☐ Friendly

FIGURE 1.5: Table tent example using *self-awareness* and *self-assessment*.

Promote Self-Awareness of Social Norms

Students need opportunities to practice social norms. Helping them to become more self-aware should be intentional. Providing students with a social norms chart can help them to be more reflective of the social norms. Figure 1.6 shows an example of such a chart. Students can use this chart weekly or monthly to see how they are progressing with social norms.

Self-Awareness	Not Yet	Working on It	All Good
Growth mindset			
Efficient			
Empathetic			
Positive			
Friendly			

FIGURE 1.6: Student self-awareness and social norms.

*Visit **go.SolutionTree.com/EL** for a free reproducible version of this figure.*

Build Individual and Group Self-Assessment Skills

When working in a group, students need opportunities to reflect on the social norms in their group. Using a group self-assessment chart after working together can help support their group. See figures 1.7 and 1.8 for samples of student and team self-assessment tools.

WE BELONG AND . . .

☐ Help one another.

☐ Show respect.

☐ Try to understand one another.

☐ Invite opinions.

☐ Use positive language.

FIGURE 1.7: Student and team self-assessment.

We Belong	Not Yet	Working on It	All Good
Help one another.			
Show respect.			
Try to understand one another.			
Invite opinions.			
Use positive language.			

FIGURE 1.8: Team self-assessment.

*Visit **go.SolutionTree.com/EL** for a free reproducible version of this figure.*

Be Aware of Bilingual and Dual-Language Instruction

The same seven steps used for preteaching vocabulary can be used in bilingual and dual-language classrooms. Take the word *crucial*, which is the same in Spanish, except for the second *c*, which is pronounced as an *s* in Spanish. In dual-language classrooms, it can be taught in either language and save half the time. For step 6, students can alternate examples in either language or use translanguaging (combining both languages in a sentence).

Adapt Preteaching for Work at Home

You can preteach vocabulary in class, and after a couple of weeks of practice with the sequence and purpose of the seven-step method, you can adapt it into a five-step process for home assignments. The five-step method is the seven-step method but without step 3, the dictionary definition, and step 5, the features of the word. It is still an effective method for preteaching vocabulary.

You can assign five words or phrases English learners need to learn before the next session as homework, encouraging students to learn them with the help of siblings or other family members. Be sure to give them the following directions.

1. Repeat the words to yourself five times.

2. Write an easy definition for each word.

3. Write an example of each word used in a sentence.

4. Complete this sentence stem for each word: _____

5. Use each word again when you read and write your assignment.

See figure 1.9 for an example of how to apply the directions.

1 Say *nevertheless* five times (to yourself or someone at home).

2 Definition: **Nevertheless** is a fancy way of saying "but."

3 Example: I want to go outside; **nevertheless**, I know I have to stay home.

4 Frame: I want to _____; **nevertheless**, I _____.

5 Accountability: Use *nevertheless* in your summary.

FIGURE 1.9: Example of five-step method.

When implementing the seven-step or five-step method, it is important to remember a few things, like timing and process. Here are a few tips to keep in mind when preteaching vocabulary to students.

- The teacher speaks for one minute. For steps 1 through 5 and step 7, the students use the word for one minute, taking turns giving examples, to generate about five or six examples each for a total of one or two minutes per word.

- The goal is for *every* student in the class to participate. Everyone practices the vocabulary in complete sentences as a class.

- Do not ask students to guess what a word means. They will spend too much time giving examples that move them away from the true meaning.

- Do not ask students to write, copy, or draw. Students will have a chance to write when they read the mentor text that serves to model sentence structures and further use of each word. Additional word study (writing own sentences, drawing representations, finding antonyms, filling in the blank) can take place later in centers, stations, or journals.

- Avoid activities or add-ons that take up to twenty minutes per word. If students spend that time reading and summarizing their vocabulary with partners, grammar and discourse will develop more effectively and quickly.

- Immediately after you teach the five words, students should use those words in their discussions, reading and summarization, and after reading in writing.

Use Vocabulary in Verbal Summarization With Peers

During teacher explanations, experiments, or when students are reading with partners, let students stop every few minutes and summarize orally with a partner what they are hearing, observing, or reading. Summarization is one of the most powerful tools for comprehension, clarification, and anchoring of knowledge. Summarization helps English learners to (1) learn and use more words, (2) describe people, places, or things, (3) identify main ideas and supporting details, (4) understand the essence and importance of the topic, and (5) verbalize ideas in order to support or refute an argument. Through summarization, students learn to use their own discourse with terms and phrases that the teacher has pretaught and many more that they learned while reading, writing, and summarizing verbally with a peer. The verbal summaries help students have clarity in discourse and organization savvy for their written summaries. Use the following six steps to teach summarization.

1. The teacher models how to summarize verbally with a paragraph from the text students are about to read.

2. Students practice verbal summarization of the same paragraph with a partner. Two volunteers share with the class, receiving feedback from teachers and peers.

3. Student pairs verbally summarize the next paragraph or demonstration and share with the class. They use the table tents strategy (page 31) in their tool kit with these words— *initially, additionally, subsequently, furthermore, moreover, finally*—to summarize in sequence. The verbal summary will help organize their writing later.

4. The teacher models how to do written summaries on the whiteboard or projector.

5. Peers practice writing a summary in the same pairs as in steps 2 and 3, volunteers share aloud, and the teacher and peers give feedback. They use the table tent for their ratiocination charts to edit their summaries. (See chapter 4, page 117, for more information on a ratiocination chart.)

6. Students finish summarizing the text individually.

When students engage in all six steps, they can present, write, and edit their summaries with confidence.

Pairing students for the summarization activity must be done with great care and *consideration* of the overall language and SEL objectives and goals set for the class. Summarization also enhances *self-management* by challenging students to be *self-motivated* and *disciplined, self-regulate*, and *self-manage* emotions by being patient with their partner. They also practice *relationship skills* by building *positive relationships* with others and *communicate positively* and clearly. As an example, all the words italicized in the previous sentence are SEL-based words students can learn using the seven steps for preteaching vocabulary (page 27). Figure 1.10 (page 36) illustrates a sample poster with guidelines for summarization that you may want to keep visible while students are working. You could also display these guidelines as a table tent.

FIGURE 1.10: Poster for summarization.

Vocabulary in Elementary Grades

Non-English learner preK and kindergarten students learn an average of three thousand words a year (Calderón, 2007b). So, teachers must be intentional about also teaching vocabulary. Teachers should select words from books, poems, songs, content areas, and SEL lessons. Elementary students learn vocabulary best when words are repeated through reading, writing, speaking, and listening. Sentence frames for elementary students should be more simplistic and easier to complete. The class can create examples to fill in the sentence frame together. Pictures are an appropriate scaffold to support elementary students as well. A fun way to engage elementary students in step 4 (when using step 4 of the 7 steps) is for students to throw a ping-pong ball back and forth to signal when it is their time to speak. In the early grades or for Newcomers there are only 5 steps and the students ping pong during step 4. SEL is embedded in this process as students work together to complete sentence frames. Figure 1.11 samples the five steps applied to the word *challenge*.

1   Say *challenge* three times (to yourself or someone at home)

2   Definition: **Challenge** is a difficult task or activity.

3 Example sentence: The student accepted the **challenge** to read more books.

4 Frame: In school,_____ is a **challenge** for me.

5 Accountability: Use the word *challenge* in your written journal entry today.

FIGURE 1.11: Example of the five-step method for elementary-grade English learners.

Preteaching vocabulary helps prepare elementary students in their discourse about the content they are learning. If they are having a discussion and the teacher asks for responses, teacher-provided sentence frames support accountable talk between the students. Students learn to listen to peer responses and add on or respectfully disagree with a peer using what is sometimes known as *accountable talk*. Some example sentence stems of accountable talk follow.

- I agree . . .
- I agree, however . . .
- I would like to add . . . I want to echo . . .
- I concur . . .
- Moreover, . . .
- Furthermore . . .
- Based on . . . I . . .
- In addition, . . .
- I respectfully disagree . . .
- I disagree due to . . .
- On the other hand, . . .

Strategies for Administrators and Coaches

When observing teachers, administrators and coaches look for the multiple ways that teachers embed SEL into the curriculum. During the seven-step method for preteaching vocabulary, administrators should see students taking turns going back and forth as described in this chapter. Administrators can also look for student engagement during summarization activities as students co-create summaries. Students may use tier 2 and 3 words to create their summaries and sentence frames, as described in step 6 of that strategy (page 27).

Coaches can assist elementary teachers with parsing texts (see chapter 2, page 54, for a discussion of parsing texts), choosing tier 2 and 3 words, and creating sentence frames for step 6 for preteaching vocabulary, as well as frames for discourse and summaries. Coaches may help to identify areas where teachers can embed SEL and provide strategies to promote SEL. Additionally, walkthrough forms should highlight the five competencies so that coaches can observe teachers to see if they are addressing the competencies throughout their lessons.

Support for Vocabulary at Home

Vocabulary practiced at home is extremely beneficial for English learners. Teachers should send newly taught tier 2 words to families by handout or email to help ensure that these words will become part of students' vocabulary. Encourage families to use the words in their discussions and in written form for homework or other opportunities like emails, cards, or journals. Families can post tier 2 words in the home as a reminder of the new vocabulary. Parent participation in step 6 for preteaching vocabulary can be helpful for the students to practice the words.

In bilingual and dual-language classrooms, teachers can assign new vocabulary words in the student and their family's home language. Family use of the five- or seven-step method or sentence frames at home helps encourage self-awareness. Sentence frames can support families to help students identify emotions, feelings, and interests, and promote self-efficacy and a growth mindset. A *growth mindset* is a cultivated belief that challenges are opportunities to improve and that one can develop all basic abilities through dedication and hard work (Dweck, 2017). Encouraging family support in teaching students to voice how they feel using appropriate vocabulary can help develop self-awareness and self-management skills. Teaching specific words for feelings, such as those listed in table 1.5 (page 39), helps students identify how they feel.

When social-emotional factors are well integrated into instructional components, teachers find that these are among the "most influential factors on student learning" (Wang, Haertel, & Wallberg, 1997).

TABLE 1.5: Emotional Specificity Chart

Happy	Angry	Sad	Good
Great	Irritated	Crushed	Peaceful
Gay	Enraged	Tormented	At ease
Joyous	Hostile	Deprived	Comfortable
Lucky	Insulting	Pained	Pleased
Fortunate	Sore	Tortured	Encouraged
Delighted	Annoyed	Heartbroken	Clever
Overjoyed	Upset	Rejected	Surprised
Gleeful	Hateful	Injured	Content
Thankful	Unpleasant	Offended	Quiet
Important	Offensive	Afflicted	Certain
Festive	Bitter	Aching	Relaxed
Ecstatic	Aggressive	Victimized	Serene
Satisfied	Resentful	Heartbroken	Free and easy
Glad			Bright
Cheerful			Blessed
Sunny			Reassured
Merry			
Elated			
Jubilant			

Source: PsychPage, n.d. Used with permission.

When integrated into the fabric of the classroom culture, climate, and academic framework, social-emotional learning creates a safe and nurturing learning environment for English learners to participate, contribute, and actively support others in the learning process. SEL improves motivation and commitment, attendance, study habits, cooperative learning, individual learning, and subject mastery (Zins, Weissberg, Wang, & Walberg, 2004).

Questions From the Field

As you might have guessed, the answers to most questions about teaching vocabulary, discourse, and self-awareness are basically the same across all grade levels, classroom contexts, and language proficiencies. If you teach in areas not highlighted here, it is highly likely that the following answers will address your questions related to this chapter's content.

 I'm an ESL teacher. How do I integrate SEL and language instruction?

Use the seven-step method to preteach SEL words and phrases. Have students interact with each other to practice the competencies and the vocabulary. Ask your co-teachers to let you know what SEL language students might need to express their concerns.

 I teach second grade remotely. How do I teach the words my English learners need for understanding core content and developing SEL competencies?

Use the seven-step method to preteach SEL words and phrases students will need. Have them interact with each other to practice the competencies and the vocabulary. Ask your English language co-teachers to let you know what SEL language students might need to express their concerns.

 I teach biology. I'm teaching key words all students need to know, but the English learners don't seem to remember them on weekly quizzes.

Use the seven-step method to preteach SEL words and phrases. Have students interact with each other to practice SEL competencies and the vocabulary. Ask your English language co-teachers to let you know what SEL language students might need to express their concerns.

Tips for Teacher Reflection and Planning

- Select five or six critical tier 2 words or phrases you want English learners to master for that class session.

- As part of daily lessons, include five or six words to preteach before reading and have students practice with a buddy.

- Ensure the texts are rigorous enough and at grade level; parse them for depth of vocabulary learning before students read.

- Provide opportunities for English learners to work in pairs for step 6.

- Hold students accountable for using new vocabulary words throughout the lesson.

- Ensure students receive SEL and ExC-ELL discourse protocols, such as tier 2 connectors or phrases, norms for taking turns, interrupting, summarizing, elaborating, accepting multiple perspectives, and so on.

- Use peer activities that strengthen valuing one's culture while also valuing other cultures and grow students' SEL competencies.

- Select performance assessments that focus on step 6 and the use of taught vocabulary throughout the lesson.

- Incorporate students' self-reflections on continuous improvement into assessments.

- Recognize where teachers need to grow in their teaching strategies and diminish biases.

Tips for a Whole-School Approach to Professional Development and Teacher Learning Communities

- Determine which professional learning opportunities would support a systemic schoolwide approach to social-emotional learning integrated with teaching language, literacy, and content in your school that would result in the explicit teaching of SEL competencies.

- Look for professional learning opportunities that support the effective use of cooperative learning activities in your school that integrate English learners into the fabric

of the school culture intentionally and enhance their
academic achievement.

- Choose professional learning opportunities that increase
  culturally responsive teaching that specifically acknowledges
  the languages and cultures of the English learner and
  multilingual learner population in your school and district.

In summary, English learners and multilingual learners will expedite
their learning with:

- More academic vocabulary for SEL, science, mathematics,
  social studies, and English language arts

- Discourse and oral summaries for all subjects and SEL

- Vocabulary to comprehend what they are about to read,
  although some may need basic reading skills (phonics,
  phonemic awareness, fluency)

- Vocabulary for writing standards and processes for different
  scientific, mathematical, argumentative, and evidence-based
  writing purposes

- Explicit vocabulary or phrases for social-emotional skills for
  effective collaborative work in pairs and teams, and to sustain
  students' own well-being

The information and instructional strategies in this vocabulary chapter serve as a precursor to reading. Vocabulary forms the foundation for building reading comprehension and rich student discussions about what they read. The next chapter elaborates on these connections and the research-based strategies for teaching reading. Chapter 3 elaborates on the use of vocabulary in oral discourse and classroom interaction. Chapter 4 carries this vocabulary into the students' writing. Chapter 5 emphasizes language for building relationships across school settings for teachers, administrators, and students.

Chapter 2

Self-Management
Applied to Reading

Key Term: Self-Management

Self-management is "the ability to manage one's emotions, thoughts, and behaviors effectively in different situations and to achieve goals and aspirations" (CASEL, n.d.d).

John was a fifth-grade English learner level 1 student. He enjoyed school and was beginning to meet many new friends. He was becoming a more fluent English speaker. He enjoyed class time, but when things became difficult, he would get off task and become impulsive. When John's impulsivity became disruptive to the class, his teacher would redirect him to stay on task.

However, when it was reading time, John was extremely focused on making progress in acquiring English. His teacher had students read and summarize in partnerships, and new English learners could read in triads. John began reading in a triad and would repeat what his partners would say. After John began to show confidence with his reading and summarizing, he moved to a partnership. The partnership was a positive experience for John. He would read his line of text and summarize with his partner. John carried this positive experience into other subjects.

Even when students appear to be uninterested in learning, they can engage when working with peers in a structured learning situation such as partner reading with summarization. This chapter focuses on that and other learning strategies that have been proven to be effective for multilingual learners, striving readers, and newcomers in particular.

Research by the National Assessment of Educational Progress (NAEP) shows that in 2021, 25 percent of all students struggle with reading, particularly in comprehension (NAEP, 2021). The NAEP results demonstrate "fourth graders have lower average reading scores than in 2017 and that scores only increased from 29 percent to 35 percent between 1992 and 2019. This crisis predates COVID-19, and the pandemic has only made things worse" (NAEP Report Card, n.d., p. 9).

To avoid perpetuating this pattern, teaching reading comprehension must begin in the earliest grades, pre–K through first grade, or as a newcomer with interrupted formal education arrives at any grade level. Keep looking to help older struggling students solve decoding problems and other early-literacy skills, and let them to ask for help if they need it. Nevertheless, all teachers can apply the easy interactive strategies described in this chapter. P. David Pearson, a reading researcher and specialist, states:

> Just because we're teaching them word recognition doesn't mean that we can't teach comprehension. And just because we're focusing on building knowledge, doesn't mean that we have to de-emphasize strategy instruction. . . We want to think of the various instructional components and activities as complementary and integrated rather than completely separated and independent of one another. (as cited in Sparks, 2021)

SEL is embedded in all parts of the reading process. The modeling of text features and structures helps with reading comprehension and prepares students to read texts. The best way for English learners to develop fluency and comprehension is to read aloud with a partner and summarize the content verbally. This chapter explores self-management in reading by reviewing the importance of SEL in reading lessons, offering strategies for planning lessons that include self-management skill development during reading, integrating literacy and SEL practices into performance assessments, and finally including some reading strategies for administrators to apply in their school districts. As you can imagine, reading is the most difficult, most embarrassing, and most dreaded instructional event for newcomers, English learners who are at higher levels of English proficiency, and even long-term English learners. To spare your students that difficulty and embarrassment, in this chapter we will teach you how to do the following.

- How vocabulary and discourse become the foundation for proficiency in reading, particularly reading comprehension
- The research-based strategies for teaching reading to English learners, multilingual learners, and all other students
- How to integrate self-management competencies into reading instruction

Students will have the tools to do the following.

- Further their word-level and syntax knowledge as they read
- Deepen word meaning in a variety of reading genres
- Use tools to discuss what they read
- Learn the content they read

Reading difficulties is a term almost synonymous with English learners and multilingual learners. The lack of quality reading instruction in the early grades has generated the largest percentage of English learners in the United States. About 70 to 85 percent of English learners are long-term English learners. Long-term English learners are students who have been in schools for six or more years and have not been able to move beyond the status of English learners because they cannot pass the exit tests. Typically, their grades have never been that good, either, and each year, their self-esteem diminishes. Self-awareness of this persistent hurdle damages their willingness and tenacity to keep on trying to do better in school. Is this the reason it seems like so many long-term English learners drop out of high school instead of graduating? The following are some of the barriers to graduation English learners face in the United States.

- They missed out on quality instruction in reading.
- They were immersed in phonics but not reading comprehension instruction.
- They were asked to read and comprehend without phonics or decoding instruction.
- The reading programs they participated in did not preteach key vocabulary that was necessary to comprehend what they were about to read.

Typically, when students arrive in kindergarten or first grade, teachers may perceive them as having a language or literacy deficit because they might not be verbally fluent in English. Thus, many teachers are reluctant to provide grade-level reading instruction that is rigorous but is fully supported with vocabulary and discourse. Without early foundational literacy skills, the multilingual learners will have a difficult time catching up to grade level. Instead of labeling them right away as limited in English, many schools now visit homes of newcomers to learn about their lives, talents, real-world knowledge, literacy practices, and the cultural norms that will help instead of hinder. Before the beginning of each school year, back-to-school preparation includes teachers going to homes. Teachers plan who visits which family so that there is no overlap.

When students read in both languages systematically throughout elementary school, they consistently outperform non-English learner peers in secondary schools.

Teachers may make another false assumption when newcomers arrive in the upper elementary grades. In this case, teachers assume that English learners have been taught to read (or decode) and so they skip teaching decoding (phonics) for even those students who need it. These gaps in reading are also the cause of so many long-term English learners in secondary schools (Calderón & Minaya-Rowe, 2011).

We know from research on dual-language instruction that knowing how to read in the first language accelerates reading in English (Calderón, Hertz-Lazarowitz, & Slavin, 1998; Collier & Thomas, 2004). When students read in both languages systematically throughout elementary school, they consistently outperform non-English learner peers in secondary schools. Their self-esteem and self-management from knowing how to read enhances their academic performance in middle and high school. In essence, the following are true.

- Teaching all the components of reading helps English learners sustain their self-esteem through the school years.

- Reading in their primary language is an assets-based approach to building self-confidence, tenacity, and reading fortitude. Looking at English learners with an assets-based lens instead of deficit-based is part of SEL. A deficit lens zooms in on what students lack. It sees multilingual learners and English learners as fragmented and needing to be fixed. An assets-based lens sees multilingual learners and English learners as valuable human beings, with rich cultures and languages, motivated and eager to learn since they overcame obstacles to get to this country (Zacarian, Calderón, & Gottlieb, 2021).

- Integrating SEL competencies and ample peer-interaction activities into reading accelerates reading proficiency in the first and second language.

Reading as the Foundation of Learning in School

Perhaps your English learners missed out on learning some of these basic reading skills. That lack has now manifested in low or average grades in middle and high school core content areas. But it is never too late! Even small doses of phonics can help. The rest of this chapter focuses on implementing strategies to recuperate the missing basic reading skills to develop depth of comprehension.

The National Reading Panel for Language Minority Children and Youth finds that vocabulary instruction leads to better reading comprehension when explicitly taught and is most effective when students have multiple opportunities to see and use new words in the

All these strategies help not only English learners but also any striving readers.

context of reading (as cited in August & Shanahan, 2006). This means that English learners need to read more and use new words throughout all reading and writing activities.

Research on How Reading Supports Learning Subject Matter

- Several studies provide insight into the impact of student engagement with text. The following shows just how important it is to begin teaching reading to students early in their learning career, because it can be challenging to do so.

- Avoiding the challenge of engaging students with texts may seem efficient, yet it ultimately undermines student learning. Instead of confronting reading problems head on, avoiding doing so breeds student dependence on the teacher for academic knowledge and places the learner in a passive role (Pearson, Moje, & Greenleaf, 2010).

- Teaching reading is one of the most challenging teaching strategies for core content teachers to cover. Yet, it is the most important learning set of strategies for English learners to meet the standards (Calderón, 2007b).

- The National Reading Panel (2000) and subsequent research panels inform us that learning to read consists of five essential components: (1) phonemic awareness, (2) phonics, (3) fluency, (4) vocabulary, and (5) comprehension.

- The Panel on Language Minority Children and Youth (August & Shanahan, 2006) reaffirms the need to teach these five components.

All these strategies help not only English learners and multilingual learners but also all readers and striving readers.

Based on the preceding research, we will take you from what to do before student reading, during reading, and after reading with activities used to anchor knowledge, language, and reading skills. First, let's see how SEL facilitates reading-skill development and how reading simultaneously develops SEL skills.

SEL Undergirds Reading

In chapter 1 (page 15), we identified multiple dimensions in which teaching vocabulary aligns with SEL competencies, specifically self-awareness. We emphasized the importance of SEL as the catalyst for understanding the value of creating a learning community that is inclusive, engaging, values the wealth of experiences and abilities inherent in diverse learners, and the need to explicitly teach SEL skills daily. Including the voices of English learners in the decision-making process of class norms for collaborative and cooperative work empowers them to believe that their voices matter and that the rules are clear, consistent, and fair. They develop these SEL competencies as they practice the seven vocabulary steps. Step 6 is their time to apply the class norms and practice cooperative learning with a peer. We emphasized that infusing SEL into vocabulary-learning activities and using vocabulary words in discourse allow students to practice and hone their self-awareness skills in a safe learning environment.

As the instructional focus shifts from vocabulary to reading, the SEL competencies that we addressed earlier are easily transferable. This is especially true as students continue working in pairs, sharing a common text, and engaging in summarization, discourse application, and verbal interaction. Talking, listening, and engaging in conversations that make English learners comfortable learning academic content will influence their attitude and motivation to want to read.

Self-management planning begins by selecting relevant materials. The benefits of experiencing mutual growth of social-emotional skills and literacy are more evident when teachers select books and materials with social-emotional content for using the partner reading strategy. Materials with SEL content that present models of adults and students solving problems and interacting have the potential to connect students emotionally with the content and the characters, real-life figures, and topics involved. Ideally, these materials also picture multilingual learners in a positive light. SEL language can also be used to describe relationships, feelings, and cooperation between objects, natural phenomena, and living organisms. When English learners have opportunities to read, speak, and write about stories or activities with emotional content and cultural reflections, their summarizations and narratives are more detailed, accurate, and coherent.

When using reading materials that have SEL content with cultural applications, English learners can better label, develop, and understand prosocial skills. For example, if the word *cooperate* is introduced during the seven-step method for preteaching vocabulary and practiced during class meetings, students can understand the

word *cooperate* cognitively and emotionally and apply it more effectively during partner reading. The self-management skills of cooperation and empathy are especially
desirable when partner reading becomes a triad that includes a newcomer with little
or no English-speaking abilities or an English learner who needs peer modeling,
specifically reinforcing the competencies of social awareness, self-management, and
relationship skills. Students and adults alike always need to practice the ability to
cooperate to learn something thoroughly.

Partner and Triad Reading Develop SEL Skills

When students engage in partner or triad reading, they not only develop reading
skills but also their emotional skills.

- **Confidence:** Reading with a partner builds confidence. The repetition
  and practice help students become more familiar with the process and
  take more risks, and encourage them to want to read more. Working
  with a partner to read and summarize can make reading a more
  successful experience, especially when texts become more complicated.
  Students can learn self-management strategies from each other, which
  will help them when reading independently.

- **Belonging:** Creating partnerships for reading provides students with
  a sense of belonging. A class with predictable partnerships provides a
  safe environment in which students feel included. They can anticipate
  with enthusiasm reading with their partner, and they do not have to
  fear that they will not be chosen or left to read on their own.

- **Kindness:** Working with a partner encourages kindness and patience.
  Students show kindness when they take turns reading alternate lines.
  When reading in a triad, they support a newcomer to read along with
  them. When creating oral summaries, they learn how to listen to their
  peers and how to add to their partner's summaries.

- **Friendship:** Reading with a partner encourages the development of
  friendships. Intentional partnering allows for students to get to know
  each other. Partnerships can turn into friendships as students read
  together daily. Flexible partnerships allow students to meet other
  members of their class that they may not have had the opportunity
  to meet. Partners learn to trust each other, and that is a perfect start
  to a friendship.

- **Support:** Reading and summarizing with a partner helps students learn to support each other. As they begin to build trust, they can help each other with unknown words or clarity in the summaries. They also can help a newcomer that may not have the English skills needed to read the words or verbalize the summaries.

- **Courage:** Reading with a partner inspires students to take risks. When they become more comfortable with reading, they can take on more challenging texts or move from alternate line reading to alternate paragraph reading. They can then eventually graduate from partner reading to independent reading and independent summaries.

- **Hope:** Partner reading aids in the difficult and frustrating experiences of learning a new language. It provides a sense of hope as partners support each other; they begin to feel more hopeful about developing literacy skills in their second language (Calderón, 2007a).

All partner reading and summarization in dual-language literacy programs, particularly when students come from different cultural backgrounds, are excellent methods for all students to develop the self-management skills of confidence, belonging, kindness, friendship, support, courage, and hope.

Reading in Classrooms Across Content Areas

Reading proficiency has been the biggest roadblock for English learners to get good grades in sixth through twelfth grades. Science projects, lab reports, mathematics, engineering problems, inquiry-based learning, or project-based learning require depth of reading comprehension and cooperative or collaborative student work.

Unfortunately, teachers often skip text reading and prefer to lecture, read to students, or assign reading for homework. Silent reading or homework reading has been the biggest detriment to long-term English learners (Calderón, 2007b; Calderón & Minaya-Rowe, 2003; Calderón et al., 2022). If English learners don't know 85 to 90 percent of the words in a paragraph or even a sentence, they won't be able to comprehend the main idea, details, or key concepts. If they don't know 85 to 90 percent of the words in a test question, they will get it wrong even if they know the concept.

That is why we started this book: to emphasize the importance of preteaching vocabulary before English learners read and the importance of students applying those words during reading to further their comprehension and knowledge of content. Teachers can also teach more words during and after reading. Arguably, more vocabulary and content knowledge made available to English learners before writing yields the type of academic writing that grade levels require. Notwithstanding all that vocabulary instruction, without applying it verbally with peers, it is not going to stick. Immediate interaction with the pretaught words is the key to learning vocabulary, reading, and writing. Teachers can use the following strategies for reading and writing across all subjects.

Strategies for Lesson Design in Reading Core Content and Learning Self-Management Skills

We tested the twelve instructional components, described in this section, that systematically build reading comprehension skills, especially those that need to be developed for newcomers or were missed by long-term English learners. As education and writing researcher Louise Moats (2020) says, "Teaching reading is rocket science." It requires exponentially more attention when it comes to multilingual learners who need to catch up to grade level or have just arrived at your school. The twelve components form the larger framework that includes basic principles of second-language acquisition, assets-based instruction, and the evidence-based components that we tested against other popular instructional models for multilingual learners (Calderón 2007b). The following twelve components for teaching reading to multilingual and English learners are also part of the professional learning model that we present in chapter 5 (page 131). Within the list, we also suggest the time you should spend on each component.

1. **Preteach vocabulary:** As covered in chapter 1 (page 15), preteaching major tiered vocabulary words for academic text will help English learners and all students feel more comfortable interacting with the text. Start with preteaching five words in ten minutes at the beginning of a class. You can teach other words as the lesson progresses. (Ten minutes)

2. **Teacher think-alouds:** Model how to use comprehension skills that students can use in the text they are about to read. (Three to four minutes)

3. **Student peer reading:** As covered in chapter 1 (page 15), pair students and have them take turns reading, alternating sentences as they read the text aloud. Voicing the text aloud with peers helps students gain confidence in their academic

voice and better retain vocabulary words they learned in the first component. (Ten minutes)

4. **Verbal peer summaries:** After the partners read a paragraph, alternating sentences for fluency, they return to the paragraph to summarize aloud what they read. There is no writing, only discussion of the most important facts, messages, and inferences in that paragraph. (Ten minutes, as part of partner reading)

5. **Depth of word studies and grammar:** Ask students to identify interesting sentences (passive voice, compound sentence) and grammatical structures (past tense) they found in the text. Then ask students to use the sentence structure they identified in their exit slip or in a composition that you will assign later in the week. (Two to three minutes)

6. **Class debriefings and discussions:** After partner reading and summarizing, have a whole-class discussion on what students found interesting, what they could relate to, or where they had difficulties understanding the subtle nuances. (Ten minutes)

7. **Cooperative learning activities:** There are many cooperative learning strategies that help anchor concept knowledge and usage of new vocabulary as students interact with other students. Chapter 3 (page 77) goes into further detail about the strategies and purpose of each. (Time varies with this strategy from three to fifteen minutes)

8. **Formulating questions and numbered heads together strategy:** Students can answer textbook or worksheet questions without too much effort or higher-order thinking. However, when students must write questions from paragraphs or larger narratives, they have to go back to the text to delve deeper into reading with comprehension. Students formulate more thinking and higher-level questions when they work in teams of three or four using strategies such as numbered heads together (see page 64). When those student-formulated questions are tested by giving them to other teams, the quality of questions improves further. (Twenty minutes for formulating, fifteen minutes for testing questions with peer teams)

9. **Roundtable reviews:** In teams of four, students take turns verbally summarizing what they just heard in a video, a lecture, or have read. They can also take turns writing down words from the text to see how many they have learned. (Five minutes)

10. **Prewriting and drafting:** Multilingual learners learn to draft compositions in teams. A strategy called *write around* (see chapter 4, page 115) can be used to draft a text-based expository composition. (Twenty minutes)

11. **Revising and editing:** Once a team has reached a certain length in their draft, team members analyze it for repetition of words, fact checking, needed evidence, or missing criteria to meet the standard. See chapter 4 (page 116) for examples. (Twenty to thirty minutes)

12. **Reading final product:** Expression and delivery of a final product is important. Students can select the medium, mode, and means for the presentation, such as a creative, colorful composition, a slideware presentation to accompany it, a role play, or another creative means. (Thirty to sixty minutes)

Begin Planning the Lesson by Parsing the Text

As an example for cross-content reading, contemporary science classrooms use complex texts that focus on inquiry, investigations, real-world data, and real-world problems. For this, teachers use a variety of texts from the internet, trade books, science articles from authentic sources such as the U.S. Environmental Protection Agency (www.epa.gov), newspapers, and some textbooks. Whichever text educators select for a lesson, they must parse that text.

Parsing a text to prepare a lesson means finding places to break up the text into meaningful chunks to then follow this sequence.

1. Select words to teach that your English learners might find difficult but are necessary to understand the rest of the lesson.

2. Select words, phrases, and questions to put on table tents (see page 31 in chapter 1) for students to use during verbal or written discourse.

3. Find words with complex spelling, phonics, or pronunciation characteristics that might need pointing out.

4. Find text features and ideas for the teacher think-aloud; identify standards and how to explain them to students and assess.

5. Find a sentence or two that you want students to emulate the construction of (syntactic features) during their writing.

6. Connect reading themes and structures to the follow-up writing assignments.

7. Use self-management characteristics to add emotion and humor to the passage by discussing relationships between words to create meaning and make connections with self, peers, self-management skills, and the real world.

Parsing a text this way goes beyond teaching to objectives or standards. Once you have parsed a text as described in the previous list, you can include the language and content objectives and standards that you plan to address.

Besides identifying standards, objectives, and key vocabulary to preteach before students begin reading, there are other instructions you can give students to help prepare them for reading.

- Highlight text features.
- Read a paragraph and point out the structure of a sentence.
- Point out the pronunciation or spelling of a difficult word you didn't include in your preteaching vocabulary set.
- Present the structure of the text.
- Add background information about the topic using text features, structures, and author's purpose for writing the text.

Use Text Features to Build Background

Instead of the teacher giving too much information, translating, summarizing a text, or using a strategy that takes the motivation away for English learners to read on their own, the teacher can do a think-aloud to model how text features hold important information that can help build background before reading. For example, use two or three text features and explain how they help students understand the key ideas in the text. These text features provide background on the topic and help students make predictions or draw interest about the topic. This text also serves as a *mentor text*, meaning it serves as a model for learning new words and for reading and writing. It becomes the source of vocabulary for preteaching; the focus of reading, summarizing, and writing to meet standards and objectives; and an exemplar for grammar, writing structures, or language usage. Any text can be used for a lesson: a chapter in a social studies text, science lab directions, a poem, song lyrics, newspaper article, or internet page.

Sentence structures can be considered text features (along with syntax or grammatical structures) because readers can immediately see the length, complexity, punctuation features, and more. You may ask students, "What type of sentence do you see repeatedly in the text?" "How long is the sentence?" "Is it a compound sentence?" and "What are two or three words that are challenging because of spelling or pronunciation complexity?" Choose one or two text features from the following list that come from the text to highlight for students.

- **Text features:** These include captions, quotations, titles, author biographies, references, charts, graphs, drawings, pictures, the reason for highlighting, bold letters, italics, sidebars, cutaways, timelines, hyperlinks, QR codes, color, and maps. Explain why they are important for the text. For example, scientific literature uses many text features to explain processes or illustrate attributes of an element. Students typically ignore these unless their value is pointed out.

- **Sentence structures:** These include compound sentences, transitions, comparisons, contrasts, supporting evidence phrases, and inferences. Some phonemic awareness or phonics within the context of teaching vocabulary or partner reading helps students remember sound-word correlation and unfamiliar words' meaning and pronunciation (for example, thorough, schema, *-ough* words).

Inform the Type of Text Structure

In addition to pointing out the utility of text features, you can also support student comprehension by pointing out the *text structures*. Authors use text structures to inform or explain information. Sometimes text structures are called *genre*. Students need to know from the start the purpose of reading a particular text and the author's intent for writing that text. Was it simply to inform? To inform about the cause and effect? To try to convince the reader about a certain point of view either based on facts or opinions? Students wonder why they are reading this text. The following are some examples of text structures you may want to share with students.

- Descriptive
- Informative
- Sequential

- Argumentative
- Problem and solution
- Cause and effect
- Claims and counterclaims
- Creative writing
- Fiction
- Historical fiction
- Biographies
- Autobiographies

Moreover, stress to students that this is a mentor text they can emulate when they do text-based writing (such as assignments in which students must defend an issue, state a claim, describe an event, or use figurative language to write their life history). After reading for a purpose and analyzing the structures that an author used, it becomes easier for students to emulate those structures as they write their own compositions. Be sure to preteach the words you want to see in their writing.

Note that your students can use table tents that contain the tier 2 words most often used in expository texts. You or your ESL team teacher can preteach two or three of those words that you think would be most useful for the reading and writing assignments. Use some of the words in chapter 1 (page 24).

Demonstrate Comprehension Strategies for the Mentor Text

To save time and make the information you're teaching comprehensible, you can integrate comprehension strategies, skills, and background building through a three-minute teacher think-aloud. The think-aloud strategy uses text features to provide valuable background information, set the purpose for reading, and emphasize more vocabulary. For example, a teacher can use a pointer on a world map and identify the colors for specific areas and countries. Figure 2.1 (page 58) gives an example of a world map showing temperature changes that a teacher could use to lead this discussion. Then, the teacher wonders aloud where the world is getting warmer and points to those areas. Following that, the teacher reads the caption below the map and makes a mistake but goes back, rereads, and self-corrects to show that self-correction is an important skill for both reading and self-monitoring.

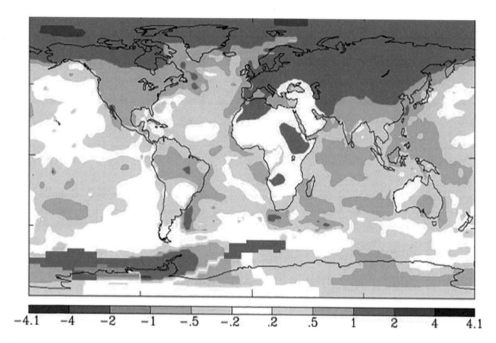

-4.1   -4   -2   -1   -.5   -.2   .2   .5   1   2   4   4.1

This map, produced by scientists at the Goddard Institute for Space Studies, shows the 10-year average (2000-2009) temperature change relative to the 1951-1980 mean. The largest temperature increases are in the Arctic and the Antarctic Peninsula.

Source: National Aeronautics and Space Administration Goddard Institute for Space Studies, 2010. Used with permission.

FIGURE 2.1: Build background—Temperature change averages from 2000 to 2009.

The teacher could then extend the lesson by saying, "I want to find out more about this. How does this relate to our world today?" The teacher would then complement the think-aloud activity with SEL language by labeling and describing emotions, shown in bold, such as *anger* at how we continue to pollute the environment, *stress* associated with the consequences of global warming, *disbelief* that some people don't believe global warming is happening, *happiness* and *satisfaction* that people are *cooperating* to find solutions to global warming, and how I should *manage* my own feelings.

After the think-aloud, the teacher can ask the students, "What was I thinking about? What was I feeling? What strategies did I use?" Keep the modeling and discussion brief. Two minutes for modeling and a two-minute discussion with students will go a long way if you ask them to use similar strategies as they read with their buddies or on their own.

Build comprehension by focusing on comprehension, not speed.

Practice Partner Reading With Verbal Summarization

From research on reading, we now know that silent reading and round-robin reading do not work for English learners, nor for many other students (Calderón, 2007b; Calderón, Espino, & Slakk, 2019; National Academies of Sciences, Engineering, and Medicine, 2017; Shanahan, 2002). The best way for English learners to develop fluency and comprehension is by having them read aloud with a partner. They need to hear themselves read in small chunks for pronunciation, reread those chunks to work on comprehension, build on both from interaction with a partner, and learn from feedback they get from peers and teachers. These processes help leverage English learners' confidence to make progress with their reading. The practice will self-motivate them to read more and help them to become more confident in their reading abilities. Partner reading helps students practice other self-management skills, such as believing in oneself, self-discipline, courage, and goal setting.

Partner reading has had one of the biggest effect sizes for underachieving students (Calderón, 2007b; Slavin, 2001). During partner reading, students read aloud in pairs and alternate sentences. They should use their *six-inch voices*, a term describing a volume level that cannot be heard beyond six inches; that way, the reading doesn't become distracting for other students. When partners alternate sentences, their brains begin to analyze sentence structures, punctuation, unfamiliar words, and reading fluency. However, this is only the first step. Partners need to go back to the paragraph they just finished to concentrate on meaning without worrying about fluency. That has already been taken care of.

The concept that fluency means reading fast has been on students' minds all these years because reading tests use timers to test reading! They still think that reading fast is reading—regardless of comprehension. This fast reading, coupled with methods that shy away from phonemic awareness and phonics, have had a tremendously negative effect on long-term English learners' self-esteem and confidence for reading. Therefore, it behooves our students when we parse the text for text features, phonics, phonemic, or syntactical (sentence) structures that might create problems for English learners. A reading or ESL teacher can help address these. The most important goal of partner reading is to create meaning with a peer. Meaning is created when we add partner summarization to partner reading after they have practiced reading for fluency, ensuring systematic discourse as part of that process.

ENCOURAGE PARTNER SUMMARIZATION

After reading alternating sentences in each paragraph, students orally summarize what they read in that paragraph. The summaries can be brief. We just remind them to try to use as many of the new tier 2 and tier 3 words they encountered. (See "Strategies for Increasing Self-Awareness in Discourse and Vocabulary Acquisition," page 24 in chapter 1.) If a text's structure is cause and effect, the partners can look for and talk about a cause or an effect. If it is problem-solution, they can talk about clues to the problem or the solution. If it is finding evidence or refuting an argument, they can determine how to support or refute an argument after reading and summarizing each paragraph.

> It's OK to do slow reading again!

Never feel guilty about the time in-class reading takes. These ten minutes of daily partner reading are teaching the students skills for life. They are learning *joint discourse*, which is critical for the workplace and college. They are learning to compromise, accept different opinions, suspend their own opinion, and develop respect and compassion. In effect, they are practicing the competencies of self-management by demonstrating their ability to be self-disciplined, resulting in perseverance and resilience. They are also practicing social awareness by demonstrating consideration for others' perspectives and opinions and a desire to contribute to the well-being of others. Additionally, students are practicing relationship skills, which complement their abilities to establish and sustain positive relationships and use teamwork to engage in academically oriented exercises. After partner reading

and summarization of the assigned text, students can write their summaries in journals. They can use cognitive organizers such as webs, drawings, and outlines, and they can elaborate by writing in their primary language if necessary.

English learners and striving readers who are non- English learners need to practice these skills daily with a partner, then practice transferring them when they begin to read independently. After several weeks of partner reading and summarization, they will have internalized many comprehension skills that they can use independently for the rest of their lives. You have taught them how to enjoy reading! When they go on to the next grade level, the partner reading and summarization must begin again with new reading skills and SEL competencies.

CREATE SYSTEMATIC DISCOURSE THROUGH SUMMARIZATION

In our studies and in the hundreds of ExC-ELL classrooms we visit, we see that when teachers incorporate pretaught words throughout a lesson, they exponentially expose students to other words they might have missed in previous school years. Use key words beyond the goal of understanding reading. When using these words to verbally summarize, students learn sentence structures, content, fluency, and comprehension. Summarization has one of the largest effect sizes for all students (Hattie, 2012). Verbal summarization with a peer or in a team prompts English learners to feel more confident when reading. Verbal summarization before writing also helps produce more cohesive and content-laden writing.

When creating summaries, students use self-management skills. For instance, students use collaboration, planning, and organizational skills to co-create the summaries. They need to remember the order and importance of the events that they read together. Working together creates a collective summary that both partners can be proud of and provides a sense of success.

Students can also practice taking initiative during partner summarizing. One partner may take initiative to start the summary, and that may encourage the other partner to take initiative on the next paragraph summary. This practice takes away the fear of taking initiative many students have. Developing courage to take initiative also carries over into other areas of learning in core content classrooms.

Partner summaries also help students set short- and long-term goals and build stamina. Partners start by summarizing single paragraphs, then pages, then chapters, and then entire books. Students and the teacher can decide together when to increase the rigor with their summaries and more rigorous texts.

It is OK to let students process information in their primary language with same-language peers. The use of two languages helps English learners reflect more deeply and find connections to their own background knowledge and culture. Additionally, letting English learners use translanguaging (code switching) shows that their home language and culture are valued in the classroom. All things considered, if teachers want to expedite comprehension in English after students process in the language of their choice, they can have English learners prepare and deliver their summaries in English. Use figure 2.2 (page 62) to show students the differences in discourses and the importance of becoming bilingual, bicultural, and biliterate in social and academic spaces where they can come and go contingent on the context.

FIGURE 2.2: Differences in discourse.

Self-Assessment or Debriefing to Anchor SEL

After partner reading and summarization, ask students to assess their partnership and their own performance. You can use a tool similar the one presented in figure 2.3.

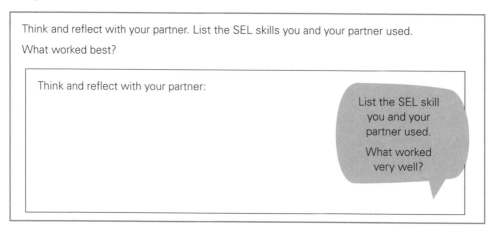

FIGURE 2.3: Think and reflect with your partner.

After you complete using reading strategies in class, employ close reading and self-assessment strategies. This will help teachers to determine whether students comprehend the text and will encourage students to self-monitor their reading.

Have Students Create Their Own Questions

What technique encompasses more information, develops more cognitive and metacognitive skills, and gets students back into the text once again to read more deeply? It is *student-formulated questions*. Writing questions is more challenging than just answering questions. Students actually have to think, discuss, and test questions with other students. In this way, students learn from one another as they work in cooperative learning teams of four to construct their questions. This is another approach to integrating language, literacy, content, and several social-emotional competencies. It is also a way to assess listening, speaking, reading, and writing. The following list shows the step-by-step procedure students should follow to formulate their own questions.

1. Students work in teams of four and use the information they have just learned from reading and summarizing.

2. Students form pairs within their teams of four. Each pair writes a high-quality question based on the text assigned to them by the teacher.

3. The team members research the answers to their questions, double checking both the questions and answers for accuracy of facts, evidence, and proper grammar.

4. Students write each question separately on the front of a card, resulting in each group of four students having two cards with a single question on each.

5. Students write the answer on the back of the card.

6. As a team, students choose a team name and write it on both cards. Later, the teacher will call the teams by team name.

7. Students give the cards with questions written on them to the teacher, who, while collecting the cards, reviews the questions and the answers.

8. After collecting all the cards, the teacher chooses four or five questions from the class to quiz them with.

How do educators assess these questions? How can students develop peer-assessment and self-assessment strategies? How do educators get students to continuously improve the quality of their questions? We suggest using a strategy called *numbered heads together*. This strategy has been around since the 1980s, but it is particularly powerful as a cooperative-competitive strategy to test the questions each team has written. This approach is particularly beneficial in helping students increase their SEL skills by being more inclusive of those who are struggling with English, strengthen their interdependency with one another to construct and answer questions, and make responsible decisions by supporting one another and taking into consideration the overall benefit to the group rather than personal gain.

The following list shows the process for conducting the numbered heads together strategy to test student-formulated questions.

1. Team members number off from one to four.

2. Everyone listens to the question under review.

3. Students discuss among themselves and find the answer.

4. Students ensure everyone in the team knows the answer.

5. Students are prepared with the answer in case their number is called.

6. Students with that number are called from four or five teams.

7. The responses must contain tier 2 and 3 connectors, transition words, accountable talk, and complete sentences to add to the responses from the other teams. You can access sample discourse cards and table tents to support this step by visiting the ExC-ELL website (http://exc-ell.com/resources).

8. The team that wrote the question serves as the *language coaches*. They take notes of the language used by those who respond, then give feedback to the responders on the language they used and celebrate their efforts.

9. The teacher debriefs with the class by asking, "What did you learn from this activity for content, process, or SEL competency?" "How did you feel?" "What would you change next time?" and "What success would you like to celebrate?"

The following is a list of example student-formulated questions.

1. What is global warming? Give a two-sentence definition.

2. What is the main cause of global warming, according to most scientists?

3. List the four consequences of global warming. Explain how each consequence of global warming that you listed could affect the environment and life on earth.

4. What kinds of weather-event changes are predicted as a result of global climate change?

5. What evidence is there that snow and ice are decreasing? Provide citations.

6. What do you think our class should do to curtail global warming?

Once students have tested their questions, those questions can become stepping-stones into larger pieces of writing, classroom debates, or further research on the topic. They can become inquiry questions for follow-up experiments or creative projects. Encourage students to practice coming up with their own questions to readings of every subject and to help them study at home.

SEL is embedded in formulating questions, the numbered heads together strategy, and feedback from language coaches. When students work together to create questions from the text in a way that indicates a high-engagement level, they are using responsible decision making and self-management. Students must work together to make decisions using planning skills and taking initiative skills. They also must create a plan for the question they co-create and the answer to the question. When they answer questions in numbered heads together, they must collectively work together to get the answer and then independently provide the answer to the teacher. This supports their independent and collective agency skills.

The language coaches get to take initiative, carefully craft their feedback not to hurt feelings, and have courage to provide that feedback. Teachers can give them table tents with polite discourse sentence starters ("I liked the way _____ stated that fact." "Although I politely disagree with that fact, I liked the way _____ ."). The team of language coaches works together to determine the feedback they will give. This role helps students practice kindness in delivering appropriate and constructive feedback to their peers.

After partner reading and summarization, ask students to assess their partnership and their own performance. Ask students to think and reflect with their partners using the following prompts.

- List the SEL skill you and your partner used.

- What worked best?

- Where do you need to improve?

Integrate Performance Assessments for Language, Literacy, and Content Learning

Data collection on authentic performance becomes easy with this integration because you can record performance for the several layers of language and literacy, as well as how much content students have learned. The following listed skills are just a few examples of items teachers can observe and evaluate in English learners' work during vocabulary and discourse learning and for reading.

- **Vocabulary:** During step 6 of the seven-step method for preteaching vocabulary, record sample sentences long-term English learners use and compare those with English learners to analyze where the long-term English learners need further assistance. Are students using word meaning correctly? Are they pronouncing words correctly? Can they give at least five correct examples?

- **Reading fluency:** During partner reading, record fluency miscues and how students used (or where they needed) the comprehension strategies or fix-it strategies you modeled and keep track over time.

- **Reading comprehension:** During partner summarization, after each paragraph, quickly note responses to such questions as, Does the student understand the main idea? Can the student identify the important details? Are English learners using tier 2 and tier 3 words to summarize?

- **Question formulation:** Review the questions students have formulated for themselves. Are the questions well written? Are they pertinent to the subject? Are the answers pertinent to the question? How much peer assistance did English learners need to complete the question?

- **Discourse assessment:** During the numbered heads together strategy, is the English learner participating in the discussion with the team to answer the question? When an English learner's number is called to answer for the team, is that person well prepared to articulate the answer? Is the answer appropriate? Does the student use tier 2 and 3 vocabulary and phrases? Does the student use those words and phrases in complete sentences? Is there a cohesive discourse between the students? Write down some examples or assign a number for

(1) emerging, (2) improved, and (3) awesome! Base your criteria for the lesson or content assessment on the examples in the next two bullet points.

- **Content assessment:** During step 6 of the seven-step method for preteaching vocabulary, are the examples the student gives connected to the content definition? During partner summaries, is it evident that the student has processed and learned the content? During question formulation, is there depth of comprehension of the subject? During the numbered heads together strategy, does the discourse reflect thorough knowledge of what the student read and processed with peers?

- **Social-emotional competencies:** During all the activities in pairs and teams, did students adhere to social and cooperative norms and SEL competencies? Did they exercise good relationship skills and self-management? What about team reflection and evaluation? Decision making? Critical thinking?

Figure 2.4 summarizes the reading process in core content classrooms grades 6–12 or upper elementary grades 3–5 to help support your lesson designs and performance assessments. Administrators and coaches can also use it as a checklist during an observation. The following items should happen during all core content class reading.

☐ The teacher parsed the text.

☐ The teacher pretaught five key words using the seven-step strategy for each word.

☐ The teacher used text features to build content background knowledge.

☐ The teacher modeled comprehension strategies students need to use for this text.

☐ The teacher explained and posted SEL competencies for partner reading and summarization.

☐ The teacher modeled partner reading and summarization with a student.

☐ The teacher debriefed and clarified the process for any student who might have had trouble following it.

☐ The students conducted partner reading and summarization for ten to twelve minutes.

☐ The teacher debriefed in-class activities, and students engaged in self- and peer assessment and partnership.

☐ The teacher and students proceeded with strategies used after reading to anchor language, literacy, content, and SEL competencies.

FIGURE 2.4: Reading process of core content classrooms.

Reading in Elementary Grades

Newcomers in elementary schools either flourish when they come with a rich literacy background, or they start to sink into a path toward long-term English learner limbo. Even students with strong primary language and literacy experiences need instruction in the five reading foundational skills: phonemic awareness, decoding, fluency, vocabulary, and comprehension (National Literacy Panel for Language Minority Children and Youth, 2006). Unfortunately, reading instruction in early grades has lacked a cohesive and intentional scope and sequence that integrates word learning with decoding skills.

Educators and publishers of multilingual learner materials rely on cueing strategies for word identification using pictures, drawing, and guessing words in context. All these cues pull English learners' attention away from decoding. They lower the chances to learn the meaning of words and to learn to read in English.

> Is this one of the reasons there are so many long-term English learners in the upper grades?

These disorganized phonics programs, while well intended, do not really teach English learners how to read. They only teach them how to guess and how to memorize lines. Students might sound like they understand when reading a sentence, but if you ask them what they have read, they won't know. By second grade, they become slow readers because the books at this level do not have enough visuals, and students do not have someone to cue them. When they get to third through fifth grades, they are low-level readers, and their comprehension skills have not developed to tackle grade-level reading. They also lack the variety of text-based listening and speaking skills they need to thrive, as well as cohesive text-based writing, spelling, and systematic vocabulary development. English learners in these environments are doomed to lower-level reading groups and will remain there year after year (Calderón, 2007b; Shanahan, 2022).

On the positive side of the spectrum, English learners flourish when they learn the alphabetic principal, phonemic awareness, systematic phonics, and decoding three thousand or more vocabulary words (in addition to the words that are being used to teach phonics). As such, phonics lessons should be integrated with book reading, having students talk about what they are reading, and writing using the new vocabulary and sentence frames they learned from the book they read.

Students benefit from partner reading and summarization in grades K–5 as well. Shared reading experiences provide an opportunity for teachers to model partner reading. When partner reading with the whole class, the teacher reads one line of text, and the class reads the next line in big books, poems, or songs. Together, they create the summary with sentence frames and starters as follows.

- This text is about _____.
- I liked _____ because _____. I learned that _____.

Subsequently, when students are comfortable, they can gradually move to partner reading while sitting together. This shared reading experience encourages taking turns and being a positive and supportive partner, and it provides a scaffold before partner reading takes place.

For formulating questions, sentence starters and sentence frames will help support elementary students in creating their questions about the text. When answering in the numbered heads together strategy, they may discuss the answers in their groups and then each repeat the answer before choosing one to say it to the class.

The list in figure 2.5 summarizes the reading process in grades K–2 to help support your lesson designs and performance assessments. Administrators and coaches can also use it as a checklist during an observation. The listed items should happen during all in-class reading.

☐ The teacher parsed the text.

☐ The teacher pretaught five key words using five steps for each word (dictionary definition and grammatical characteristic are not necessary for K–1).

☐ Teacher taught the alphabetic principle, phonemic and phonological awareness, vocabulary, and how to bring all this together to decode.

☐ Teacher used text features to build content background.

☐ Teacher did a read aloud to model fluency first, then again for English learners to read along.

☐ Teacher read a third time to model comprehension strategies students need to use for this text.

☐ Teacher explained and posted SEL competencies for partner reading and summarization.

☐ Teacher modeled partner reading and summarization with a student.

☐ Teacher debriefed and clarified process.

☐ Students conducted partner reading and summarization for ten to twelve minutes.

☐ Teacher debriefed and students did their own self-assessment and partnership.

☐ Teacher and students proceeded with after-reading strategies to anchor language, literacy, content, and SEL competencies.

FIGURE 2.5: Reading process in grades K–2.

Strategies for Administrators and Coaches

There are many things administrators and coaches should look for in English learner reading lessons. When observing a reading lesson, they should look for interactions during partner reading. Students will be sitting side by side or knee to knee and taking turns reading alternate lines. They should observe students working in pairs or triads to co-create summaries after each paragraph. The teacher may have sentence frames and starters to support the students in their summaries. The flow stems from the explanation of SEL competencies for working together, staying on task, and developing reading skills.

When students formulate questions, administrators should look for students working collaboratively in groups of four to create questions. Table tents with sentence frames and verbs may be visible at each station or posted in the classroom.

During numbered heads together, administrators may observe students working together to discuss the answer to the posed question and then individual students responding with an answer to the class. They will notice language coaches listening to the answers and providing constructive feedback to their peers.

Coaches, similarly, can work with teachers to do the following.

- Have students pair up for partner reading.
- Observe pairs during reading and provide the teacher with feedback on how the partnerships are working.
- Decide when pairs are ready to move on from alternate line reading to alternate paragraph reading.
- Observe formulating questions and numbered heads together and document how groups are working together and if all students are contributing.
- Provide suggestions for sentence frames on table tents.
- Support teachers in identifying ways in which they can incorporate SEL competencies into the lessons.

Support for Reading at Home

Educators can offer families formal workshops on how to support reading at home. Share how families can practice some of this chapter's strategies at home. Reading to and with a child in the home language has great benefits, as does reading at home in general (Berk, 2013). One benefit is that the whole family can get involved. Partner reading can continue in the home when grandparents, parents, and siblings read together with the student in the primary language or English. Family members and their child can alternate reading lines of text and summarizing at the end of each paragraph or page (Calderón & Minaya-Rowe, 2003).

When adults read to children, discuss story content, ask open-ended questions about story events, explain the meaning of words, and point out features of print, they promote increased language development, comprehension of story content, knowledge of story structure, and a better understanding of language, all of which lead to literacy success (Berk, 2013). In addition to these benefits from reading, when adults read to the children in the home language, it develops pride in the home language; moreover, it develops biliteracy.

Families can also practice the strategy of orally summarizing after watching a show or movie together. A pause-and-summarize strategy every fifteen minutes will help enforce summarizing skills. The idea of synthesizing and summarizing can be carried into many home experiences.

Questions From the Field

Naturally, teachers will have many questions about the complexities of teaching an English learner to read. Please see the following questions for some helpful guidance on how to navigate common issues that come up.

Should I wait to teach reading to my English learners until they start speaking English?

Never! It will only hold them back. Your English learners can handle listening, speaking, reading, and writing if you support them with SEL motivational competencies and quality reading instruction.

How do I begin the process of integrating SEL with reading?

English learners need the five foundational reading strategies supported by teaching vocabulary early and aggressively intertwined with SEL. They should start with simple books to learn the protocols and routines but must be reading grade-level books by the end of second grade or in upper grades after a year.

I'm afraid to use partner reading alternating sentence by sentence with my high school students. How can I make it work?

Follow the process described in this chapter. From interviews and observations, we found that high school students love partner reading, especially for Advanced Placement courses. It helps them dive deeper into comprehension and content mastery. They cover more content territory faster too.

Should I translate or find translations for my second graders so they can understand what we will be reading?

It is not necessary to do so. They can read if you preteach five words, and they read and summarize with a partner. Translating will make them dependent on receiving translations. Do give them permission to process information in their primary language but have them report in English.

I tell my English learners during round-robin reading to look at the pictures and guess the words. Is that scaffolding OK?

It is not OK. This is too much cueing or sheltering, which prevents English learners from putting effort into decoding. Make sure they are decoding rather than guessing with those cues, which are not scaffolding, only stifling. Show students how to sound out letters in a word and decode, not guess.

I'm an English language teacher and I never took reading courses in college. How do I help my co-teacher?

You can help by preteaching tier 2 words and phrases from the text English learners are about to read. Parse the text to see what English learners will need to master for other classes.

How do I help my English learners tackle challenging texts in science and social sciences?

Implement the complete process described in Strategies for Lesson Design in Reading Core Content and Learning Self-Management Skills (page 52): model comprehension strategies with think-alouds, partner reading and summarization, and after-reading cooperative learning activities to anchor language, literacy, and content. You will see how these strategies impact English learners' and other students' reading.

Should I let my English learners discuss content in their primary language?

Yes. Discussing concepts, clarifying questions, and synthesizing in the primary language helps English learners understand the concepts. Peers can help report their knowledge in English. Preteaching some key words will help students' verbal and written discourse even more. After studying and implementing reading and self-management strategies, the whole school can move forward to more targeted discourse skills. Chapter 3 (page 77) elaborates on discourse and the social awareness skills that foster academic interaction.

Conclusion

As you explore several strategies to increase reading proficiency, such as teacher think-alouds, partner reading, and question formulation, it will become increasingly apparent that the self-awareness strategies utilized with teaching vocabulary also apply to reading. The utilization of self-management pairing strategies that focus on building relationships will make partner reading safe, motivational, and academically enriching. Associating reading with social interactions with other students that English learners trust and enjoy working with will enhance their confidence as readers. These positive experiences, integrated with specific strategies to increase academic language, will further prepare English learners to read and comprehend more challenging and complex text and be better prepared to write with greater fluency.

1. Preteaching of Vocabulary
2. Teacher Think-Alouds
3. Student Peer Reading
4. Verbal Peer Summaries
5. Depth of Word Studies and Grammar
6. Class Debriefings and Discussions
7. Cooperative Learning Activities
8. Formulating Questions and Numbered Heads Together Strategy
9. Roundtable Reviews
10. Prewriting and Drafting
11. Revising and Editing
12. Reading Final Product

Tips for Reflection and Planning for Teachers and Coaches

- Make reading in class for at least ten to fifteen minutes part of daily lessons.

- Ensure texts are rigorous enough and at grade level and parse them for depth of reading.

- Provide opportunities for English learners to work in pairs, teams of four, or project-based teams for summarization, ample discussions, and peer feedback.

- Ensure students receive SEL and ExC-ELL discourse protocols, such as tier 2 connectors and phrases, norms for taking turns, interrupting, summarizing, elaborating, accepting multiple perspectives, and so on.

- Design peer activities so that they grow students' SEL competencies, including valuing one's own culture while valuing the cultures of others.

- Select reading materials that include culturally relevant content.

- Formulate after-reading activities that provide students opportunities to produce high-quality work.

- Focus performance assessments on vocabulary, summarization, and partner reading discussions.

- Incorporate students' self-reflections and team reflections on continuous improvement into assessment.

- Recognize where teachers need to grow in their teaching strategies and diminish biases.

- Ensure all teachers have access to SEL standards and indicators so that they can explicitly teach and embed SEL competencies into their lessons.

- Equip teachers with strategies and materials that facilitate intentional grouping of students into teams and pairs that accelerate their learning.

Tips for a Whole-School Approach to Professional Development and Teacher Learning Communities

- Work for full commitment by everyone at the school to English learner success.

- Shift to an asset-based mindset to recognize how much English learners have learned at home in the year.

- Build relationships with families and become partners with them.

- Create a policy for the use of home-language literacy in learning to read.

- Teach parents ways to have ample discourse with their children, including vocabulary, songs, family histories, sayings, idioms, jokes, reading to them, and encouraging them to read.

- Strengthen cultural connections by having educators visit students' homes and learn about their cultures. Educators then connect what they find with instruction by providing students with books that represent them and the cultures educators observed in students' homes.

- Emphasize phonics and decoding.

- Assure mainstream teachers that they have all the tools to effectively accelerate reading in their subject areas.

- Ensure everyone has clarity about what is equity and what is not: there is clarity of actions and conceptual clarity.

- Move all students in a similar direction to ensure grade-level reading for English learners.

After studying and implementing reading and self-management strategies, the whole school can move forward to implementing more targeted discourse skills. Chapter 3 elaborates on discourse and the social awareness skills that foster academic interaction. Students need to articulate their thoughts about a topic with peers to clarify, expand, and process key facts and opinions before they start to write. Therefore, we propose delving deeper into teacher-student and student-student interaction practices before contemplating writing formal, creative, or text-based compositions.

Social Awareness
Applied to Discourse

Alaina was a high school junior and English learner. She loved coming to school. She loved her community of English learner friends. However, Alaina did not like to speak or present in front of the class. She was self-conscious of her accent and felt like everyone stared at her.

Alaina was in a history class with a teacher that used lots of whole-group instruction practices and spent a lot of time lecturing to the class. Alaina tried to follow along, but the teacher spoke fast and used a lot of terms that she did not understand. She did her best to pass the class but the tests were hard and no matter what she did to prepare, she still fell short on the grade. She grew frustrated and checked out.

The history teacher also assigned a lot of presentations. Alaina did not want to present in front of the class. She was afraid to ask her teacher for another assignment, so she just didn't do it. The teacher met with the English language teacher and said that Alaina was just not doing anything in his class and she probably would not pass the class at this rate. The English-language teacher-provided suggestions for the teacher, but at this point, he had given up on Alaina. End-of-year report cards came, and Alaina did not pass the class or the state exam. She'd have to take the history class again.

The following year, Alaina had a different teacher for history class. This teacher did things differently from day one. Students worked in groups a lot and had many opportunities to talk about what they were learning. The teacher provided prompts for discussions, and Alaina looked forward to each class. The content was still difficult, but she had opportunities to process the information she was learning. As a result, she became interesting in learning about history. The end of the year came, and this time, she not only passed the class, but she also passed the state exam.

Alaina experienced the type of classroom barriers that stifle language development: asking English learners and multilingual learners questions in front of the whole class, ineffective instructional practices, and a teacher who misunderstood her struggles.

Typically, teachers ask students to jump from reading a text right into writing. When this happens, students don't have opportunities to connect deeply with a text. They might not even process important ideas, details, or facts, or form opinions. Processing information entails ample discussion with peers for testing, validating, expanding, debating, or developing knowledge beyond a superficial basis.

SEL and Academic Discourse

During the COVID-19 pandemic, many students received instruction virtually. During virtual learning, students mostly listened and read, but opportunities to speak were lacking. So, it is not a surprise to see that the 2020 World-Class Instructional Design and Assessment scores showed little growth in speaking in grades 5–12 and negative growth was double for grades K–1 (Sahakyan & Cook, 2021). In *Examining English Learner Testing, Proficiency, and Growth: Before and Throughout the COVID-19 Pandemic* (Sahakyan & Cook, 2021), researchers at the Wisconsin Center for Education Research remind us that talking is still one of schools' great challenges. Virtual learning allowed students to disengage and did not encourage them to talk about their learning. Many students kept their cameras off and typed in the chat box instead of unmuting. This learning gap has impacted student growth with speaking.

Couple the lack of speaking with the rise in mental health issues and students keeping many of their struggles secret from caretakers and educators. Isolation and interrupted schooling brought on depression, anxiety, and panic attacks. As a result, these mental health issues have impacted student learning and achievement. The American Academy of Pediatrics (AAP), American Academy of Child and Adolescent Psychiatry (AACAP), and Children's Hospital Association (CHA) have declared a national emergency in children's mental health, citing the serious toll of the COVID-19 pandemic on top of existing challenges (AAP News, 2021).

Teaching social-emotional skills is hard, time-consuming, and necessary. However, educators can teach SEL skills throughout the day within each subject instead of only teaching skills in isolation (Cohen, Opatosky, Savage, & Stevens 2021). Learning SEL skills starts with students having ample opportunities to talk with peers and teachers using the kind of language scaffolds that we share throughout this book. Students need to talk to adults, peers, and their family members. Planned discourse in the classroom helps promote communication in students. The more opportunities to speak, the more educators can help students meet their needs. Speaking is integral to student growth academically, socially, and emotionally. Opportunities for discourse help students feel more welcome, accepted, and included. Discourse also provides a way for students to be able to discuss what they are experiencing. So, what does that mean for teachers?

Teachers need to be intentional about providing opportunities for students to speak, especially since students grew accustomed to not speaking during virtual learning. In fact, they might not have spoken much before. We know that English learners who have been in the United States for six or more years and are still labeled long-term English learners were probably sitting quietly in the back of the room or also perceived as shy and ignored.

To overcome past inequities, teachers should strategically plan activities to encourage discussions throughout a lesson. If students are not talking to each other, they are not fully processing what they are learning. To truly understand what they are learning, students need to use all four domains of language: (1) speaking, (2) listening, (3) reading, and (4) writing. This chapter shares ways of using peer interaction, after-reading activities to delve deeper into reading comprehension, and higher-level academic discourse for students to master the content they are studying. In this chapter, you will learn how discourse benefits SEL and vice versa, how cooperative learning supports SEL across all content areas, and how to integrate SEL into discourse development, along with practical advice on discourse development for elementary teachers, administrators, and families.

When students engage in conversations, they get to practice SEL competencies. These include social awareness and relationship skills. Specifically, engaging in discourse supports hearing and understanding perspectives, demonstrating concern, empathy, and compassion, and displaying gratitude. Students learn to take turns speaking and listening and learn how to respectfully agree or disagree. They can find validation in discussing what they learned. We know that when someone teaches something to someone else, it validates what the teacher knows. Giving students opportunities to discuss what they are learning with a peer can reinforce learning. This process can go back and forth and help foster confidence in learners by instilling social awareness skills.

Engaging in discourse also helps students see the perspectives of others. Hearing others' ideas can help students see how their peers learn and process, which can help them learn to empathize and be more compassionate. They may learn that other students have similar experiences to their own and may see that they are not alone in their thinking.

Working with other students helps students see the strengths in others. If only a few students talk in a class, other students will not have opportunities to show their knowledge or unique abilities; they may come to believe their ideas don't matter. Giving all students time to talk helps them see that their opinions and ideas matter. It also helps the class to see that everyone has something to contribute.

Finally, to learn English, English learners need opportunities to talk and listen. They need to hear their peers talk. They need a safe space to practice speaking English. Requiring English learners to speak in front of the class without the chance to rehearse can be intimidating and harmful. The experience can cause trauma to the English learner and may discourage them from talking. English learners, especially newcomers, can speak about their learning but they need partners or small-group opportunities to do that in. Talking, discourse, interaction—whatever we choose to call it—is critically important for multilingual learners, English learners, and newcomers.

The Research on Peer Interactions and the Benefits

Research shows a clear connection between healthy peer inter-actions and increased self-confidence and social awareness. The following is a list of facts detailing the positive effects of including discourse development in the class curriculum.

- David W. Johnson, Geoffrey Murayama, Roger T. Johnson, Deborah Nelson, and Linda Skon's (1981) meta-analysis and Robert E. Slavin's (1989) best-evidence synthesis find that cooperative learning, in comparison to competitive and individualistic learning, has very strong effects on achievement, socialization, motivation, and personal self-development.

- Students will likely achieve more and develop more positive relationships if teachers structure students' academic goals cooperatively early on in the school year. Further, educators and students alike will begin to associate higher levels of achievement with more positive peer relationships (Roseth, Johnson, & Johnson, 2008).

- There is overwhelming evidence that cooperative learning as a pedagogical practice has had a profound effect on student learning and socialization (Slavin, 2014).

- Placing students in groups and expecting them to work together will not necessarily promote cooperation. Group members often struggle with what to do. Discord can occur as members grapple with the task demands as well as managing the processes involved in learning, such as dealing with conflicting opinions among members or with students who loaf and contribute little to the group's goal (Johnson & Johnson, 1990). It becomes even more difficult for English learners with the added stress and tasks for learning English (Calderón, 1993).

Cooperative Learning Support for Social Awareness in All Content Areas

Scholars David W. Johnson and Roger T. Johnson (2009) propose structuring positive interdependence within the learning situation so all group members understand they are linked together in such a way that one cannot achieve success unless they all do, and they must learn to synchronize their efforts to ensure this occurs. However, assigning students to groups and expecting them to know how to cooperate does not ensure this will happen. When groups don't work well together, it's often because they lack the interpersonal skills required to manage agreements and disagreements among group members. Teachers should negotiate cooperation and collaboration skills with older students and teach those skills to newcomers and younger students. The benefits of cooperative learning are as follows.

- Greater motivation to learn
- Increased academic achievement
- Improved metacognition
- Better problem solving
- Better sense of belonging in class and schools
- Better multicultural relationships

While some initial attempts at cooperative learning may feel awkward or uncomfortable for students, they can experience all the aforementioned benefits over time. Apply cooperative learning consistently in the classroom and students will quickly see improvement in their social awareness skills. Because there are many benefits for cooperative learning, teachers must teach students how to work in cooperative groups. This includes modeling expectations for what the group should look like and sound like. Use a fishbowl method (described on page 91) to have a group model the expectations so students can analyze the modeling and develop norms for engaging in the cooperative groups.

Integration of SEL, Peer Interaction, and Learning

There are several skills students must learn to be able to successfully collaborate with their peers. Some of the following are learned in relation to other students and others are individual skills students must learn on their own in order to work better with others.

- **Interaction competencies:** These competencies form from having positive interactions with others and address how to encourage, help others' efforts, accept help, share ideas and resources, provide feedback, challenge conclusions to complete the task, and meet group goals.

- **Individual accountability competencies:** These competencies include accepting one's responsibility for completing their individual share of the work while also ensuring that others complete theirs. Students must feel personally responsible for contributing to the collective effort of the group while curtailing any anger or frustration that derive from disagreements.

- **Reflection, self-evaluation, and group evaluation:** Successful cooperative learning is accomplished through group processing, which involves students reflecting on their progress and their working relationships.

- **Learning to learn skills:** When students engage in high-level cognitive talk, which incorporates task-related talk about facts, concepts, thinking, and making sure the content is learned, they become better able to self-direct their own learning while contributing fully to group efforts.

We prefer to call the work students do in small groups *teamwork* instead of *group work*. Teamwork is more like sports, where everyone depends on one another yet each is also independently accountable. In our experience, teams of four work best. More than four students tends to be too many and some students will use the numbers to disengage from the group. Three is too few and runs the risk of two students partnering and one being left out. The pairs that work together during step 6 of the seven-step method for preteaching vocabulary, like providing a sentence frame for students to orally practice in pairs, during partner reading, and during summarization activities can join another pair and form teams quickly.

Teachers strategically assign teams. Ideally, the teams are heterogeneously composed of different ethnic backgrounds, mixed abilities, different levels of English proficiencies, and gender. English learners benefit from these teams much more than sitting together with those who speak the same preferred language as them all the time. There are times, though, when English learners can work together using their preferred language for certain activities. However, varying those times is more beneficial to learning English. Table 3.1 clarifies what teamwork does and does not entail.

TABLE 3.1: The Principles of Teamwork

Teamwork Is	Teamwork Is Not
• Using the language of cooperation that was explicitly taught • Applying high-level discourse to process information • Delving deeply into the task • Ensuring everyone is learning • Ensuring interdependence and individual accountability • Forming heterogeneous teams	• Providing unstructured turn-and-talk time between adjacent peers • A teacher sitting next to an English learner as they do their individual assignments • Translating for an English learner instead of teaching or facilitating learning • Engaging in a superficial approach to the task • Sitting together in a team while one student does the work for others to copy • Putting all the English learners together in one team

The five SEL competencies are built into cooperative learning, but social awareness is the most relevant competency. When planning to have students work in teams, establish the norms of interaction or SEL competencies for that assignment. As aforementioned, educators can set the expectations for the groups and a group can model for the class. From the model group, the students can create norms. This can be done as a class or within the small groups. Once the class creates norms for cooperative groups, each individual group can assess to see which norms they follow well and which norms they may need to practice more. The following are some examples of helpful interactions between students.

- **Use active listening with each other:** Active listening includes looking at the speaker, paraphrasing, and asking questions to show the speaker you are listening.

- **Share ideas and resources:** Ideas about books, articles, content, and more can be shared with the group. Students can respectfully agree or disagree with the comments.

- **Comment constructively on others' ideas:** Provide feedback that will help support or enhance a student's work. In writing, students can provide constructive feedback, such as suggesting adding details to a sentence to provide more information.

- **Accept responsibility for one's behavior:** If a student does not display positive behavior or makes a poor choice, their team members prompt the student to own their mistake and move forward.

- **Make decisions democratically:** This can involve taking a class vote or the consensus of the class.

After teamwork, whether completed or to be continued, the team can use a rubric to gauge the quality of their collaboration and the quality of their product. Figure 3.1, figure 3.2 (page 86), figure 3.3 (page 86), and figure 3.4 (page 86) offer some examples. However, encourage students to come up with their own social norms and ways of evaluating by first having them brainstorm from a list of competencies, choosing the ones they think would help their teams be *effective, efficient,* and *successful*! Be sure to teach the meaning of these words. When students work in a team, they should assess how the team members interact. Then show them the examples from this chapter. Charts like those that follow can provide a framework for students to gauge what the team does well or what the team needs to work on to be more productive. These charts, such as figure 3.1, include team and self-reflections for students to use.

Team Assessment Form

Team name: _____

Date: _____

Team Norm	Need to Work on It	Almost Awesome	Awesome Accomplishment Because . . .
Listen actively to each other.			
Share ideas and resources.			
Accept responsibility for one's behavior.			
Comment constructively on others' ideas.			
Make decisions democratically.			
Learn the content.			

FIGURE 3.1: Team assessment form.

*Visit **go.SolutionTree.com/EL** for a free reproducible version of this figure.*

We did well on the social skill of _____ when _____
_____.

Other places we could use the social skill of _____ could be
_____ and _____.

We could improve our use of skills _____ to better
learn the content.

FIGURE 3.2: Reflection statements.

Visit go.SolutionTree.com/EL for a free reproducible version of this figure.

Question	Response
What have we achieved?	
What do we still need to achieve?	
How might we do this?	

FIGURE 3.3: Sample team reflection questions.

Visit go.SolutionTree.com/EL for a free reproducible version of this figure.

My Role	Need to Work on It	Almost Awesome	Awesome Accomplishment Because . . .
Did I contribute?			
Did I help someone who needed help?			
Did I make the best use of my time?			
Did I listen to others' points of view?			
Did I learn the content?			

FIGURE 3.4: Self-awareness form.

Visit go.SolutionTree.com/EL for a free reproducible version of this figure.

The team and individual norms will continuously change. Once the students have accomplished a competency or skill that they can remove from the charts, they can add a new competency to work on. The forms can be used in various ways. Students can glue the forms into their journals and reflect often about their group experiences, or students can complete the forms as an exit slip for the teacher to view and utilize for making instructional decisions.

Teacher Assessment of Cooperative Learning

Observation and feedback are the most powerful tools to assess student learning. You might want to walk around with the same checklist or rubric you've provided to students (or custom forms they created) and record your observations, focusing on one or two teams at a time. Collect the students' self- and team-evaluation forms and match their findings to yours. If you find that a team is struggling to work together or some are not participating, you can plan to spend time with that group and model how to work as a cooperative group. If you find many groups are struggling, you can discuss as a class ways to improve group participation and use a group that is working well together to model for the other groups. The other groups can take notes on what the group is doing and share their findings with the class.

At the same time, it's necessary to assess how well students learned the content they studied together through quick formative assessments like exit slips or similar brief written or verbal summaries. Exit slips are a great way to assess student understanding and mastery. At the end of the lessons, teachers can provide a prompt or question for students to answer. Teachers can use this as a formative assessment and sort the responses into groups for students who have mastered a concept and can receive instruction to deepen their learning or students who have not yet mastered the concept and need reteaching or additional support.

Content mastery is the end goal. The way to assess English learners' needs for accommodations is contingent on each student's overall language and conceptual growth. Plan to have multiple ways to assess English learners' knowledge acquisition of course content, such as providing bullet lists and graphic organizers and giving them the option to choose verbal or written or illustrated work. Set up short-term and long-term goals. Give feedback to students on a daily or weekly basis. Feedback should be specifically related to a concept or goal to lead students to mastery or to extend their learning.

Have brief debriefing sessions with the whole class after a complicated activity. English learners will benefit from listening to other non-English learners who were also wondering about specifics. The whole-class debrief can help support all students.

Strategies for Integrating SEL in Discourse Development

Instead of reteaching vocabulary or other skills that English learners and peers might have missed the first time around, there are many different cooperative learning strategies that teachers can use to further develop student discourse, enhance learning by processing information at a deeper level, and demonstrate student strengths. The following strategies are intended for use in any content area.

Four Corners

The teacher chooses four different discussion questions about the content students are learning. The teacher places the discussion cards in each corner. The teacher assigns students to each corner. The students go to the corner and discuss the topic for the allotted time. One student shares out what the team discussed.

This strategy supports the social awareness competency by helping students see different perspectives about a topic. It also supports relationship skills by supporting effective communication and teamwork. This strategy supports English learners by ensuring they have a small team to practice communication skills with.

Vocabulary Buddies

Tier 2 vocabulary buddies is a quick way for students to meet with a partner to discuss their learning. Students receive a card with a list of five to ten tier 2 words on it (*subsequently*, *notwithstanding*, and *effect* are good example words for this exercise); content-specific words work well too.

To begin, students write the names of different classmates next to each word on the list. When the teacher wants the students to talk about a topic, the teacher directs the students to take out their tier 2 vocabulary buddy sheets. Then the teacher announces a word and tells the students to go with that buddy. The words and buddies can change with each unit. Having this system ensures that students always have a partner and don't have to go looking for one. It gives students an opportunity to meet other students in the class that they may not have met before. It supports social awareness by hearing from peers and getting different perspectives and relationship skills by working as a team and supporting peers.

Inside-and-Outside Circles and Concentric Circles

Divide the class into two equal groups. One group makes a circle and faces out. The second group makes a circle around the other circle and faces in. This should set students up to be in partnerships. Students discuss a topic with their partner. The teacher sets a timer for the time that the students should discuss the topic. The outer circle then steps to the right, and each student ends up with a new partner. The teacher can play music during the transition to add an element of fun.

A variation of this strategy is to form a conga line rather than circles. One group stands in a line parallel with the other group. As in inside-and-outside circles, the two lines should set students up to be in partnerships. The partners can discuss the topic, and then one line takes one step to the right to make new partnerships. The concentric circles and conga lines set students up in partnerships so that they can discuss the topic with a peer. This strategy supports social awareness and relationship skills through students learning about other perspectives, supporting peers, and practicing effective communication skills. See figure 3.5 for an illustration of these circles.

FIGURE 3.5: Inside-and-outside circles.

Categorical Lineup

The teacher poses a line order to the class. For example, students line up in order of their respective birth month. Then starting with January birthdays, students stand in line according to where their birthday falls. Then students figure out where to stand in the order, so each says their birthday as they go in order down the line. It's always fun to see if there are any duplicate birthdays. Then once in line, students count off by the number of groups the teacher wants, and the students sit together in those groups. So if the teacher wants seven groups, the January birthdays start with one and when it gets to the seventh student, it will start back at one. Then all the students assigned ones get together, twos get together, and so on. This strategy is great for pairing up random groups of students and helps support social awareness. Students could be in a group with classmates they may not normally work with, providing them an opportunity for seeing different perspectives.

Roundtable Summaries

Have students sit in groups of four. After reading or participating in a lesson, students summarize what they learned verbally as a group. This could be at the end of the day or the end of a lesson. The teacher provides sentence starters, such as *first*, *then*, *next*, and *last*, to guide the summary then moves to more challenging transition words as the year progresses, such as *initially*, *following that*, *subsequently*, and *finally*. The teacher may provide table tents with the transition words and starters or have them on a slide or poster for all to see. This strategy supports relationship skills as students have to work as a team by listening to what was already said and to add to the summary.

Table Tents as Discussion Frames

During teamwork, have table tents with the sentence frames listed in figure 3.6 for team discussions. Having table tents available helps students who may need the language to engage in the discourse. These tents can have starters, questions, phrases, or key words to help support the discussions. Remove these scaffolds once students display an understanding of how to engage in the discourse.

Asking for information	I'd like to know . . . Do you know . . . ? I'm interested in . . . Would you tell me . . . ?
Requesting confirmation	If I understood correctly . . . In other words . . . Does this mean . . . ?
Interrupting	Excuse me . . . Sorry, but . . .
Illustrating	For example . . . For instance . . . Moreover . . .

Agreeing	I concur . . .
	I agree . . .
	I agree and would like to . . .
Disagreeing	I politely disagree . . .
	However, the author states . . .
	On the other hand . . .
Making suggestions	Why not . . . ?
	Why don't you . . . ?
	Let's . . . . Have you thought about . . . ?
Giving reasons	Additionally . . .
	Furthermore . . .
	Moreover . . .
Giving opinions	I think that . . .
	In my opinion . . .
	I'm sure that . . .
Correcting yourself	What I meant was . . .
	What I mean is . . .
	Let me try again . . .
Checking for understanding	Did I get that right?
	Did you understand?
	OK?
	OK so far?

FIGURE 3.6: Frames for team discussions.

*Visit **go.SolutionTree.com/EL** for a free reproducible version of this figure.*

Discourse in Elementary Grades

Students as young as preschool should engage in discourse with their peers. Students can learn how to respond with sentence frames and sentence starters in all subject areas. These starters can provide them with a scaffold to engage in discussions.

Students can turn and talk with their elbow buddy (person sitting next to them) during any lesson to summarize what they are learning or to pose questions to each other. Model this process to the whole class and practice it with partners. The students can peer reflect and the teacher can observe and provide feedback. Then the class may observe a pair of students engaging in the discourse with the fishbowl method. The *fishbowl method* is an organized discussion strategy in which students in a class are organized into two discussion circles: an outer ring and an inner ring. The students in the inner circle, or the fishbowl, lead a discussion among themselves while the students in the outer circle listen. Afterward, students discuss what they observed and provide feedback. The class may also create norms for engaging with partners based on what they observed. The following are examples of cooperative learning across disciplines in elementary schools.

- In shared reading with teachers, students summarize what a teacher reads after each page or a brief section. Teachers ask students to use as many words from the shared reading as possible.

- In partner reading, students discuss parts of the book they are reading. Together they summarize what they are reading or what the teacher taught the class. Identifying common themes and character development are good topics for discussion.

- In science and social studies, students discuss what they read or what the teacher taught. They reflect on science labs or discuss historical events. Reflections on learning are good practices for processing information.

- In mathematics, students discuss how they solved a problem or other possible solutions to a problem. The justification process provides students with an opportunity to reflect on what they did to get the answer and see other possibilities based on what their partner says.

- In writing, partners share ideas and orally tell their stories or topics before they write, edit, and revise together.

Strategies for Administrators and Coaches

Coaches and administrators should look for multiple opportunities throughout a lesson for teachers to encourage students to talk about their learning. They should monitor the percentage of teacher talk to student talk. If the teacher is on the stage for a large percentage of time, student understanding and achievement suffer. In a 2019 study, researchers observed 639 ninth-grade students to see if the amount of teacher talk versus student talk affected student achievement, finding a positive link between individual participation and achievement in all students (Sedova, Sedláček, Švaříček, & Majcik, 2019).

Coaching teachers to get off the stage can be challenging, as many believe that they are the content experts and that students will not learn the information if a teacher is not teaching it directly to them. Therefore, starting slow and small is important.

Sharing a strategy with teachers such as vocabulary buddies (page 88), orally summarizing (page 90), or four corners (page 88) can be a great starting point. After implementing the strategy, the coach and teacher can discuss the results, focusing on the goal of seeing better gains when students have more time to discuss their learning.

Support for Discourse at Home

Providing intentional discourse opportunities in the home language helps students practice conversing with others about a topic. Discussions about what to pack for lunch or what to wear to school are great examples of places where families can use discourse at home. Families can use starters such as, "How can we add vegetables to your lunch today?" or "It is cold today. What might you wear to make sure you are warm?" Those starters can spur on conversations and discussions in which students can voice their opinion in a respectful way and respectively listen to other perspectives. The family member and student can come to an agreement after both sides are heard and understood.

Families can practice the skills of social awareness by engaging in games in which they take turns and respectfully win or lose. Video games, board games, and card games all provide opportunities for families to model good sportsmanship and teamwork.

Questions From the Field

Making SEL intentional and part of the curriculum takes time and reflection. Teachers have many questions about how to strengthen teamwork and group work. See the following questions for samples of what educators often ask about social awareness and discourse.

My English learners won't engage in conversations in mathematics or history class. They do well on the exams but won't talk about the content with their peers when I put them in a small group. What can I do to encourage discussions with English learners?

English learners want to talk with their peers about their learning, but it can be intimidating and overwhelming. However, with modeling, practice, and scaffolds, English learners can engage in discourse with peers. Before structuring teams, post social norms such as the following.

- Help those who need help.
- Respect one another.
- Everyone contributes.

Monitor the teams as they work and redirect where necessary. Ask students to self-assess as individuals and as a team.

 My newcomers are very shy and want to work alone. How can I help them become more sociable?

Have a conversation with the English language teacher. Teachers that work with such students should plan how to create safe spaces for them to use words and phrases that you have given them to practice before the time to use them. Continue for two weeks to help develop self-confidence. Also pair newcomers with a native English speaker to repeat what they are saying until they feel comfortable using sentence frames.

 I tried cooperative learning because it is supposed to help students learn subject matter and many skills, but it didn't work. What should I do?

This happens to many teachers. Be sure to start with the social norms and competencies. Begin with pairs, moving on to teams of four, and use whole-class strategies such as vocabulary buddies. Provide ample modeling, practice, and feedback. Periodically have teams that are effectively working together model their teamwork for the class. Students can take note of what is working and practice that in their own team. The team can reflect and discuss if it worked.

 What are some ways I can help multilingual learners become aware of the strengths they bring?

Teachers can assist students with making a profile or autobiography. The profile can include drawings, pictures, artifacts, and words or phrases students already know. It can also include an interview of interests and strengths. When students feel like they cannot do something, the teacher can direct them back to their profile or autobiography to remind themselves of what they can do and build on that. Have students share their profile with a peer and ask that peer to add positive characteristics they observed about that student. Students can also ask family members, student teams, and the entire class to share more positive characteristics.

Conclusion

English learners need explicit instruction that integrates language learning, literacy, core content areas, and the social-emotional skills that will facilitate all learning. The integration is applied by English learners and classroom peers when cooperative learning is the vehicle to practice speaking, listening, reading, and writing in pairs or in small teams of four that are carefully orchestrated by the teachers. There are specific opportunities for pair practice, such as vocabulary practice during step 6 of the seven-step method for preteaching vocabulary (page 27 in chapter 1) and during partner reading with summarization. A myriad of teamwork opportunities comes after partner reading that helps to anchor knowledge. We shared some in this chapter.

The cooperative learning strategies in this chapter are intended to be used mainly after partner reading. Some, such as vocabulary buddies, can be used for class building or team building at the beginning of a class period. However, most are to be used after students have worked in pairs.

For pairs or teams to work effectively, social-emotional discourse and protocols for working together should precede any activity. The students adhere to these social norms much better when they are part of the decision making of what will work best for their team. Taking a few minutes to reflect on their performance and achievement after working together helps students develop empathy, respect, self-awareness, and self-management. Working together intensifies positive relationships and appreciation of their teacher and school.

Tips for Reflection and Planning for Teachers and Coaches

- Review the five CASEL SEL competencies and their attributes.

- Parse your lesson's material to select words to preteach.
- Identify the competency's vocabulary and sentence structures you will teach.
- Identify the competency you want students to apply.
- Use the cooperative learning strategies during the twelve lesson components.
- Model samples of the social norms to share with students; teach that language to English learners.
- Preteach vocabulary, partner reading and summarization, and the social norms that go with each.
- Offer rubrics to students to self-assess.
- Monitor teamwork, assess, and give constant feedback to English learners.

Tips for a Whole-School Approach to Professional Development and Teacher Learning Communities

- Provide schoolwide professional development on cooperative learning.
- Parallel to that, provide schoolwide professional development on social-emotional competencies.
- Follow up the professional development with coaching individual teachers to support their implementation.
- Follow up with teacher learning communities in which teachers discuss how to integrate SEL, social norms, and self-awareness with cooperative learning structures and the content they will teach.
- Teachers and administrators meet to review and find policies and structures that need to be revised in order to effectively implement evidence-based integrated instruction.
- Explicitly teach classroom norms of interaction.

- Preteach key words related to SEL competencies for an activity and words for understanding the task, peers, and content students will be processing.

- Explicitly teach the five SEL competencies and give examples of how to use them during each learning activity.

- Provide more cooperative learning opportunities to enable more student talk, develop social-emotional skills, and improve relations among diverse students.

- Offer choice in team strategies for learning in STEAM subjects and project-based learning.

- Offer choice in self- and team-evaluation rubrics.

After studying, discussing, and implementing discourse opportunities for students to enhance their academic language and social interaction skills, the class can move on to writing instruction. By now, even English learners at the emerging English level can write because they have been pretaught key vocabulary, used that vocabulary during discourse with peers, and read texts with information on the topic of the writing assignment. They now have language and information to use for writing and a high level of comfort in their writing ability.

Chapter 4

Responsible Decision Making Applied to Writing

Key Term: Responsible Decision Making

Students with **responsible decision-making** skills make "caring and constructive choices about personal behavior and social interactions across diverse situations," which "includes the capacities to consider ethical standards and safety concerns and to evaluate the benefits and consequences of various actions for personal, social, and collective well-being" (CASEL, n.d.d).

Kristine was a middle school student who had just been reunited with her mother after seven years apart on two different continents. She had also been reunited with her sisters, who had already been in the United States for a few years. Kristine attended a private school in her home country and now entered a public school system. The school placed her in a general education class with support from an EL teacher. The class was diverse and had several English learner students who were from various countries. Kristine entered the class with hopes and dreams of continuing where she left off in her country. She excelled there and wanted to excel here in the United States. She knew her limitations with the little English she had learned at her old school, but her ambition was strong and she knew she would do well.

Kristine found herself extremely frustrated after the first week. She did not feel welcomed in her new school. Her teachers were kind and warm, but she felt uncomfortable around her peers. Their stares, comments, and questions made Kristine feel isolated and alone. She decided that even though they acted that way, she had goals and dreams and she was not going to let those students get to her.

After a few months in the school, the tension with the other students mounted. She appreciated the times she went to English language class with only English learners. However, when she was in the general classroom, the discomfort continued. Her teachers did their best to address the issues and would move seats, have class circles, and try to restore the relationships, but those same students would find opportunities to get to her. Kristine started to get angry and began fighting back. Kristine would shout at her peers and call them names like they would do to her. She started coming to school on guard and angry every time she entered.

Then, Kristine's English teacher began a writing unit with the class. Students went through the writing process and then worked together to edit and revise their pieces. Kristine found comfort in being able to express herself in writing at her pace and then share those ideas with her peers in small groups. In the small groups, students shared their stories. The power of their stories broke down some of the barriers they were putting up. As the writing unit continued, Kristine started to engage with those students in a more positive way and began to feel more comfortable in her classroom. This started her love for writing and provided an outlet for her frustrations.

Although Kristine's teachers tried moving desks around and have class circles for students to share their feelings, these actions didn't address the problem for a bright student like Kristine. When the writing unit called for working in small teams, the students' engagement improved. Kristine and her peers received the responsibility of turning out a great piece of writing together. This meant making many smart decisions on how to tackle the assignment, work together effectively, and edit and revise not only the piece of writing but also their behavior toward the team. Of course, the teacher laid out some social norms and task completion suggestions, but the final organizational and interactional decisions were up to the team.

The Value of Social-Emotional Competencies in Writing

SEL undergirds writing. We discussed in chapters 1 (page 15) and 2 (page 43) how embedding SEL in vocabulary and reading instruction is a sure formula for creating proficient readers while building the competencies of self-awareness and self-management. In chapter 3 (page 77), we looked at how social awareness competencies help students practice discourse in their new language as they interact and build relationships. The next step is to transition English learners to skilled writers based on the mentor text they just read. This is where the teacher's abilities in scaffolding the positive climate and culture of inclusion and support, as well as academic skills, will be put to the test. Writing for English learners cannot be an isolated, disjointed exercise that the teacher only scrutinizes for grammatical and syntactical accuracy. Instead, writing needs to be an engaging and collaborative interaction between thoughts, emotions, environment, and peers for the English learners. For long-term English learners who have not been successful or even challenged to write, these first steps to get them engaged in writing can be highly emotional, stressful, anxiety ridden, and terribly embarrassing.

This is where student voice and repeated practice of class norms of collaborative and cooperative work empower English learners to feel more confident about taking on the task of writing.

Therefore, in this chapter, we outline a productive method for integrating writing into the English learner's journey through SEL-based language learning and by building on vocabulary, reading, and discourse skills reviewed in previous chapters to help students use responsible decision-making skills in their writing practice. Like the engaging SEL strategies used with vocabulary and reading, you can use the guidance in this chapter to support English learners in working in interdependent teams, writing a common text, using discourse and verbal interaction around the initial writing samples, and engaging in editing for the final product. The process is sequential, collaborative, and ensures 100 percent participation. In the process, English learners will practice many of the SEL competencies, particularly responsible decision-making skills, and every student will be able to produce a writing sample from day one, without exception or excuses.

Writing as a Means of Access or a Barrier to Opportunity

Writing is a complex and challenging task to teach and learn. However, it is essential that students become fluent and competent writers. Writing can serve as either a means of access or as a barrier to opportunity. Those who write effectively have an advantage in applying to college, seeking employment, or earning promotions. They can also use writing to think through ideas and assimilate new information in the core content classes.

English learners come to school with diverse writing skills, multiple languages, grammars, cultures, and community literacy practices. Little is written about how English learners learn to write and how best to teach them how to write. However, we found in our work at Johns Hopkins that writing strategies work best with English learners when they are taught in the context of what they are reading and as they use the new vocabulary and sentence structures they have learned. We found that expository or content-based writing is easier for English learners than literary writing after a teacher takes them through all the before-, during-, and after-reading activities discussed in previous chapters. Expository texts (like science, social studies, mathematics) have a systematic vocabulary corpus and sentence structures that make it easier to emulate when writing about the topic. However, literature comes alive when it reflects English learners' culture and interests and leads to writing their own life histories. This type of writing is more subjective, and different students will need different vocabulary and sentence structures.

We also found that setting a climate of cooperation in the classroom is vital for the writing process to function. In the past, it was easy to ask students to jump into writing or to work in groups without establishing norms, protocols, and expectations for team behaviors and performance. Without integrating SEL competencies and frequently reminding students to use and self-assess these competencies, the team writing will derail or water down.

A good avenue into writing for English learners that helps foster a climate of cooperation and challenges them to exercise their decision-making judgment is content-specific writing.

In our BCIRC and ExC-ELL studies, students' writing showed huge improvements with this comprehensive approach. English learners showed they could analyze and synthesize content as well as make responsible decisions from sources they read to present careful analysis, well-defended claims and ideas, and clear information. They drew evidence from a text or texts to support analysis, reflection, or research.

Effective writing instruction gives students frequent opportunities to write with peers, accompanied by feedback and opportunities to revise and edit, along with guidance on how to do so. Instead of dictations, short-answer activities, and other similar tasks that limit writing practice, educators need to provide examples of various writing genres and discuss their individual attributes, purposes, and formats so that students can see and understand the differences (Calderón, 2020).

> **Content-specific writing** focuses on generic conventions and vocabulary specific to the subject, models what counts as evidence, and demonstrates organization of the genre in a given topic or format: lab report, newspaper article, project report, engineering plan, and other disciplinary types of writing.

Throughout the year, students' writing should demonstrate increasing sophistication in all aspects of language use, from vocabulary and syntax to the development and organization of ideas, as they learn to work with increasingly demanding content and sources.

Writing for content learning treats writing like as a tool for learning content material (Graham & Perin, 2007). Since English learners and low academic-level students are in core content classrooms most of the day, all students should receive daily opportunities to do expository writing. To be considered expository, a sample of writing must meet the following criteria.

- The work presents a main point and supports that point with concrete evidence.
- The work is contingent on the ability to analyze and explain.
- The work shows relationships between ideas and concepts.

- The work involves making a claim or taking a position while supporting it with details and evidence.
- The work is logically organized.
- The work has complex sentence structures and connectors (Graham & Perin, 2007).

Writing can help English learners understand, process, and think critically about content information. They need to read first to learn about a given topic or subject, discuss with peers to evaluate their own understanding of the topic, and then use that information for writing.

The Research on Teaching Writing

The following are facts and researched strategies for implementing writing in a classroom with English learners present.

Writing, according to the National Council of Teachers of English (2008), can be "a gatekeeper because those with weak writing skills face limitations on what they can achieve in schooling and the world of work" (p. 4).

It may be that writing on lab worksheets is less supportive of meta-cognitive skill growth and comprehension because it is potentially a less active process than discourse and summary work. Summarizing requires more active transformation of understanding because students must construct new representations of the text (Pearson, Moje, & Greenleaf, 2010).

Establish writing routines that create a pleasant and motivating writing environment (Graham & Perin, 2007). Create routines that ensure that students write frequently. Design instructional routines in which students compose together. Establish goals for students' writing (Rogers & Graham, 2008).

Implement a process approach to writing (Graham & Sandmel, 2011; Hillocks, 1986). Process approaches teach writing by engaging students in a step-by-step sequence of planning, drafting, revising, editing, and publishing (or completing) compositions in multiple genres.

Writing wings is an approach to teaching writing in which students work in writing teams to help each other through writing process activities. Students help each other plan, draft, revise, edit, and publish compositions in various genres such as personal narrative, contrast, comparison, business letter, and persuasive arguments (Slavin, 2019).

Student Team Reading and Writing is a cooperative learning program for middle schools in which students work in four- or five-member teams to help one another build reading and writing skills. Students engage in partner reading, story retelling, story-related writing, word mastery, and story structure activities to prepare themselves and their teammates for individual assessments and compositions that form the basis for team scores. Instruction focuses on explicit teaching of metacognitive strategies. Education researcher Robert J. Stevens (2003) evaluated Student Team Reading and Writing in high-poverty middle schools (grades 6–8) in Baltimore and found a significant positive effect size of +0.38.

In the BCIRC, elementary English learners engage in explicit instruction of vocabulary, partner reading, summarizing, and story-related writing. Elementary dual-language students made great gains with this process (Calderón, Hertz-Lazarowitz, & Slavin, 1998). The ExC-ELL model for secondary students had the same components (Calderón, 2007b).

Based on these facts, the following sections offer recommended best practices for educators of English learners to apply to planning writing lessons in their classrooms, including expository writing and creative writing.

Teaching English Learners Expository Writing

Approach English learner writing in a holistic fashion for best results, from vocabulary to discourse to reading and writing. Grammar should be taught in context by pointing out sentences in the text. Exclusive focus on grammar distracts students and teachers from the wider range of writing features and benefits. When teaching English learners expository writing, please remember the following items.

- English learner writing consists of pulling words, phrases, and sentence structures from the mentor text.

- English learners need to read and learn different text structures and genres.

- English learners benefit from the phases of peer drafting, editing, revising, and peer and self-editing.

- SEL competencies are taught during each phase of the writing process.

- After learning drafting, revising, and editing techniques with peers, English learners' individual writing improves.

- After practicing all the steps on paper, English learners' use of computers for writing assignments will also show more engagement and motivation to produce writing of greater length and quality.

In all core content classes, teachers should remember to do the following.

- Parse the reading text.

- Preteach five key words using the seven-step strategy for each word.

- Use text features to build content background.

- Explain and model comprehension strategies, text features, and text structures students need to use for this text.

- Explain and post SEL competencies for partner reading, summarization, and collaborative writing.

- Model partner reading and summarization to the class with a student.

- Debrief and clarify process questions.

- Have students conduct partner reading and summarization for ten to twelve minutes.

- Ensure students complete self- and partnership assessments.

- Proceed with after-reading strategies to anchor language, literacy, content, and SEL competencies.

- Recognize that English learners (even newcomers) master more vocabulary from all these steps and are now ready to write.

Planning Writing Lessons

Begin planning the writing lesson by completing the following listed steps.

1. Configure students in teams of three or four (no more than four).

2. Present the social and cooperative norms and the self-assessment rubrics.

3. Give students five minutes to review the text they have been reading.

4. Have students write a first draft (how to write the draft and steps 6–9 of this list are described in Strategies for Writing and Responsible Decision Making, page 111).

5. Have students select one composition to ratiocinate (explained on page 117).

6. After ratiocination, ask students use the cut-and-grow strategy (described on page 119) to revise.

7. Encourage students to write a powerful conclusion and title.

8. Provide time for students to do one final edit.

9. Create a forum for students to publish or present their written work.

The write-around strategy explained in this chapter (page 115) begins with prewriting lessons and immerses the students in drafting, editing, revising, final editing, and sharing in the context of a truly supportive learning community. Throughout the writing process, English learners weave the knowledge of the newly acquired tier 2 vocabulary words and increased comprehension of text

> Can you think of the SEL competencies English learners would learn from this process?

from partner reading to co-create a writing sample that they will own and develop. Since this process is not done in isolation, English learners engage in conversations, comparing each other's work, exchanging ideas to learn from one another, and assisting each other to edit and produce a final product. As a scaffold, use an attention-grabbing poster, table tent, or bookmark, such as the following example in figure 4.1.

Social Norms for Today

Everyone contributes

Help others

FIGURE 4.1: Poster for a day's social norms.

Writing Is Social and Emotional

Instead of overwhelming English learners with grammar and rigorous writing rubrics, divide the multiple dimensions of writing into procedures that are safe, simple, and structured, allowing students to become aware of their own social-emotional skills, particularly decision-making skills, and the connection to writing. For this to happen, teachers need to rehearse the procedures for the write-around strategy and allow students to practice several times and not give up after a few times.

Teacher skill at dividing students into teams of three or four is an SEL process. Just as with step 6 of the seven-step method for preteaching vocabulary (page 27) and with partner reading (page 59), the assembling of compatible teams cannot be left to chance nor does the practice of self-selecting work for all students. Building good relationships between teachers and students and between students and students is dependent on teachers making critical and proactive decisions that are in the best interest of all students, a win-win for English learners as well as for high achievers. English learners need to trust their teachers will help them learn and not leave them to fend for themselves. Building trust is just as important as teaching content. English learners appreciate simply having a caring adult listen to their efforts and the content of their writing is less important at the beginning.

Responsible Decision Support for Writing In All Content Areas

Text-based and creative writing are part of responsible decision making because students demonstrate curiosity and open-mindedness; identify solutions for personal and social problems; evaluate the consequences of their actions; reflect on their role to promote personal, family, and community well-being; evaluate personal, interpersonal, community, and institutional impacts; and recognize how critical thinking skills are useful both inside and outside of school.

Writing doesn't always have to be technical. It could begin with affording English learners the opportunity to become familiar with the process of writing by practicing creative writing about what is familiar and relevant to their own personal experience. Students can then graduate to more expository writing skills.

English learners can also write their histories, feelings, concerns, and special interests in various formats such as poems, raps, posters, fliers, blogs, scripts, and other creative representations. Newcomers can incorporate visuals to complement their poetry, songs, or plays with peers. Writing can and should be fun and effective for all students so as to engage them in the collaborative writing process (Calderón, 2007b), as long they are given the vocabulary and mentor text models to emulate. The following are some SEL-focused projects for creative writing.

- Letters to oneself or to friends once a month
- Notes to parents, grandparents, or teachers
- Blogs
- Digital slide presentations (Microsoft PowerPoint, Google Slides, and so on)
- Photo journals
- Mini webpages
- Artwork and narratives like comics and graphic novels

SEL themes in creative writing include the following.

- A conflict between two characters
- A strategy for dealing with bullying
- An autobiography
- One of the following prompts:
  >> *A person I saw in a movie . . .*
  >> *My family's hometown . . .*
  >> *My family's history . . .*
  >> *Describe a parent or relative . . .*
  >> *What I see on the way to school . . .*
  >> *A happy story . . .*
  >> *Everyone has unique talents . . .*
  >> *Abilities . . .*
  >> *Individual strengths . . .*
  >> *I believe in myself because . . .*
  >> *I can handle challenges . . .*
  >> *How I deal with anger, or a conflict, or fear . . .*

Co-Teaching by ESL Teachers and Core Teachers

Content teachers also have mentor texts for students to emulate when writing. Some English learners may also be learning from English as a second language classes, English language development, or sheltered English instruction teachers. If that's the case, teachers can begin to teach the process of writing by using an easier mentor text. The text can use words and sentences that are not as complex as grade-level texts but it must contain enough meaty content for students to find inferences, cause and effect, evidence, and any other skill the content teacher might be working on this week or next. If possible, the mentor text can be in the students' home language. The key is to make the writing process the central focus and avoid having students struggle through unfamiliar language and routines as they internalize the writing strategies.

If both English language teachers and content teachers are co-teaching in the same classroom, both can monitor and support the student teams during the first few trials. Around the third time teachers use a writing strategy, such as the write-around strategy (page 115), students know what to do and begin to become self-reliant.

In addition to content-based mentor texts, teachers can also use creative writing with topics of interest to the English learner, such as "Who am I?" "My long journey," and "Mis cosas favoritas." As students write on one of these or a topic of their choice, it is still important to display connectors, transition words or phrases, and other vocabulary that might come in handy. Be ready for students to bombard you with question like, "How do you say _____?" Your other option is to allow *translanguage* as a stepping-stone to English. Translanguaging is fine for drafting, poetry, or other creative endeavors. However, students feel accomplished when they can write a complete composition in one language. Just like summarization with a buddy, English learners benefit from extensive brainstorming aloud with a partner.

Whatever text teachers select, co-teaching can set the foundation for the writing process. In case there is no opportunity for co-teaching, mathematics, science, engineering, social studies, and language arts teachers can collaborate around interdisciplinary projects, such as a STEM project, together with the English learner in mind. The strategies that follow in this chapter focus on integrating discourse, reading, writing, and content learning along with SEL.

Strategies for Writing and Responsible Decision Making

The National Academies of Sciences, Engineering, and Medicine (2018) call for providing students with opportunities to actively participate in tasks science and engineering experts routinely engage in. The goal is to have all students participate, including English learners. The STEAM practices include the following.

- Asking questions and defining problems
- Developing and using models
- Planning and carrying out investigations
- Analyzing and interpreting data
- Using mathematics and computational thinking
- Constructing explanations and designing solutions
- Engaging in argument from evidence
- Obtaining, evaluating, and communicating information

Figure 4.2 shows samples of models and symbols of design across science, engineering, and medicine in image form.

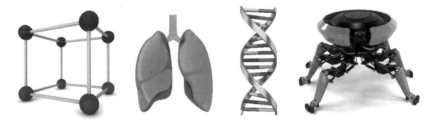

FIGURE 4.2: STEAM images.

Begin STEAM With Interaction

For STEAM, language development begins with knowing how to ask questions. First, educators teach or model for students how to ask powerful questions to investigate a phenomenon. To facilitate this when preparing to show a video on the topic, have question stems or sample questions on table tents for students to practice as you show the video. Stop the video every three minutes or so and have students turn to a partner and verbally ask a few questions about what they saw on the video. Next, ask for a couple of partners to share their questions. They can hold the table tents in their hands as they share their questions. Students can use the following sequential questions to discuss videos in class.

1. What is important in this video?

2. What evidence do we have to support that idea?

3. Do we need more information?

4. What connections can we make to our own interests?

5. What connections can we make to our own lives or cultures?

Inform students that they cannot repeat the same question. Tell them you plan to call on several volunteer student pairs to share their questions and answers. If you think you will have reluctant volunteers at first, assign numbers to the pairs and pull out numbers at random each time you stop the video. As they begin to read and gather ideas, they can use sentence frames such as the following.

- I think _____ because . . .

- I think there is supporting evidence on page _____.

- I would like to add that . . .

- I can explain that this way . . .

- I think that relates to . . .

- The evidence that supports my argument is . . .

Use Inquiry-Based and Assets-Based Learning

Inquiry-based learning is an assets-based approach that works well with English learners and multilingual learners because it is a great way to engage students in self-discovery (a responsible decision subcomponent). English learners and multilingual learners in inquiry-based learning know their voice matters to the teacher. Having choices motivates and empowers English learners and multilingual learners because they are studying things they care about. It helps them develop a deeper understanding of concepts as they learn key language, literacy, and SEL skills. It is an assets-based approach because it makes learning accessible to a wide range of students with a wide range of languages and proficiencies.

Inquiry is an ongoing iterative process that enables multilingual learners to display their knowledge, curiosity, and hidden talents when they get to choose their questions and lines of inquiry as well as the language of their choice or translanguaging. During each phase, they are learning how to learn. Once they have sufficient information, they can concentrate on drafting, editing, revising, and using as much academic language as possible.

Adopt the Collaborative Writing Process

Once students have read a mentor text, watched videos on the topic, or taken a field trip to further their knowledge on the topic, they are ready to start drafting a composition. The approach to writing begins by working in teams of four to go through this writing process.

The collaborative writing process steps are as follows.

1. **Discussions before writing:** Students talk among themselves about the topic they will be writing on to gain a better understanding and share information with each other. This step is imperative for English learners' comfort and reflection on the content.

2. **Drafting:** All students in the team should participate, even newcomers. Students should use a strategy such as write around to draft because it holds all students accountable for writing when their turn comes.

3. **Editing:** Once the team has drafted ideas into a one- or two-page document, students can begin the editing.

4. **Revising:** After the first editing with ratiocination, students revise with the cut-and-grow strategy (page 119).

5. **Writing a powerful introduction, conclusion, and title:** Once students have edited and revised the composition, they need to add a purposeful introduction, a powerful conclusion, and then an attention-grabbing title.

6. **Sharing and finalizing:** The team decides how they will share the final composition with the class, the school, or the community.

STEP 1: PREWRITE AND BUILD BACKGROUND WITH DISCUSSION

Before students write, they watch videos, gather information, and amply discuss topics, themes, opinions, and connections to their own cultures. Assign students a text to analyze for this activity or a new text on a similar theme. This will become the mentor text. Use the mentor text to point out the following six items.

1. Tier 3 words
2. Transitions with connectors and transition words
3. Tier 2 clusters ("Over the course of . . .")
4. Sentence structures
5. Beginning sentences in each paragraph
6. Conclusion types

Use table 4.1 to introduce information about writing. You can also post this information on students' table tents.

TABLE 4.1: Explain the Text Type and the Author's Purpose

Text Type	Purpose
Persuasive Building arguments, writing argument essays, problem-solution essays, editorials, public-service announcements, responses to a prompt, and so on	To change the reader's thinking, move the reader to action, or convince the reader to accept the writer's explanation of a problem or concept by supporting claims with clear reasons and relevant evidence
Informative Explanatory writing: process essays, definition essays, comparison-contrast essays, cause-and-effect essays, responses to a scientific explanatory prompt, and so on	To examine a topic and convey ideas, concepts, and information through the selection, organization, and analysis of relevant content in order to increase knowledge, explain a procedure, or explore a concept in depth
Narrative Writing account of connected events, storytelling, chronicling, taking an account, and so on	To entertain, instruct, or inform by developing real or imagined experiences or events using effective techniques, relevant descriptive details, and well-structured event sequences
Personal Summarizing, paraphrasing, and quoting, writing research reports, and so on	To share one's own life stories, topics of interest, or creative writing dealing with oneself or social awareness topics
Research Journal writing, using learning logs, writing blog posts, emails, tweets, and so on	To record observations, thoughts, conclusions, questioning of information, sharing information, asking for information

Source: Calderón, 2020.

Identifying and teaching the purpose for writing helps students understand the audience and what areas they need to address in the writing piece. The teacher can preteach vocabulary related to the piece and provide mentor texts for students to view and use for creating their own pieces. Use table 4.2 to help students find the purpose for their writing.

TABLE 4.2: State the Purpose for Writing

Text Structure	Purpose
Problem and Solution	To show the development of a problem and one or more solutions to the problem; the author states a problem and various solutions or uses a question-answer format and addresses the problem
Compare and Contrast	To point out likenesses (compare) or differences (contrast) among facts, people, events, or concepts
Cause and Effect	To show how facts, events, or concepts (effects) happen or come into being because of other facts, events, or concepts
Description and Definition	To address a specific topic and its attributes and provide main ideas supported by rich and descriptive details
Sequence and Reference	To provide information or list events in chronological order and present details in a specific order to convey specific meaning

Source: Calderón, 2020.

STEP 2: DRAFT IN TEAMS USING THE WRITE-AROUND STRATEGY

Long-term English learners want to think, write, and shape arguments the way scientists, mathematicians, historians, and other changemakers do. To help develop English learners and all students into effective writers, we suggest educators use a strategy called *write around* to have students draft their individual compositions in teams of three or four (Calderón, 2020). Once each student in the student teams has drafted a page or so of content, they then edit, revise, and add an introduction, conclusion, and title, in that sequence.

When introducing this strategy, remind newcomers that they can use their primary language or use translanguaging when they need to in the drafting stage. During the editing stage, they can change what they want or what the teacher and peers suggest. These are the steps for drafting in teams using the write-around strategy.

1. Students clear their desks. The teacher provides a prompt for all students.

2. Each student on the team needs one sheet of paper and one pencil. Each team member copies the teacher-provided prompt on their sheet of paper, completes the sentence, then passes the paper to the right.

3. Each student reads the sentence on the paper they just received, writes one additional related sentence based on the previous sentence, and passes the paper to the right.

4. Students read all previous sentences and add another related sentence each time they receive a new sheet, then pass it to the right. As students add to the work, they use tier 2 and 3 vocabulary from the mentor text in the sentences they contribute.

5. Students continue passing papers around and writing until they fill at least three-quarters of a page or full page, double spaced. However, writing may continue beyond this point, concluding only when the teacher says to stop.

Students can pull their desks together in quads or triads or even in straight lines as some computer rooms have been set up. With iPads or other tablet devices on their desks, they can write a sentence and pass the tablet to the right for the next student to add a sentence. With computers in a straight line, the students move from one computer to the next for several rounds.

Just as with paper and pencil or online, the tablets and computers can make writing exciting by using the same routines and constant back and forth discussions with peers.

STEP 3: EDIT THE DRAFT

After determining students have written sufficient sentences by walking among the groups as they work, the teacher calls time. Students then take turns, each one reading aloud to group members the composition that they have in their hands. There are no specific individual owners of the writing, as each team member has contributed to each paper. After reading, students either work with all four papers in their group to revise, or they choose one of the papers on which to focus their revisions.

Students need to choose a strategy where they revisit their writing in order to make their compositions better. Explicitly model the strategies you want students to choose between, providing English learners with systematic steps for editing and revising all their writing. The following sections include some viable strategies for revision.

Edit With Ratiocination

Ratiocination is a logical, step-by-step process to circle, underline, square, color-code, analyze, evaluate, and rework one's writing. Using ratiocination, teachers model for students how to apply specific skills in context, focusing on the use of specific elements of language. However, students are responsible for checking their own papers, thus reducing the paper load for the teacher! Most importantly, students are responsible for identifying elements they need to change or improve. During the phases of writing, students learn to cooperate, offer assistance, accept assistance, and become self-directed. Figure 4.3 reviews basic ratiocination steps.

Code	Revision choice
Draw a box around the first word or phrase of every sentence. Make a list of all the first words in each sentence.	Can we change any of these words to more sophisticated transition words, phrases, or connectors?
Circle the verbs.	Are verbs in the correct tense? Would a more active verb fit here?
Underline repetitive tier 1 words.	Can we substitute repetitive tier 1 words with tier 2 words?
Underline each sentence with an alternating color.	Underlining alternating sentences shows structure and length variety. How might we combine or break apart different sentences?
Look for gaps in the text.	Where do we see passages with a lack of evidence, fuzzy ideas, or other ways the text is unclear? What adjustments, additions, or other changes can we make to fill gaps?
Here is something for you to look for in your writing.	(As the teacher, add one feature to this space for a student who needs extra practice in areas of writing such as punctuation, capitalization, verb usage, and other skills.)

Source: Calderón, 2020.

FIGURE 4.3: Ratiocination chart.

*Visit **go.SolutionTree.com/EL** for a free reproducible version of this figure.*

Distribute a table tent for ratiocination. Two cells are blank so that you can add specific needs for this assignment or differentiate and highlight a specific task to one team or student. Maybe each team is working on something different, and these blanks will help to differentiate.

Teachers need to explicitly demonstrate and model both the strategy of ratiocination and the SEL competencies that students will use before they start to write. After that, ask students to apply ratiocination only on items that they have practiced and learned. As they work on a draft, if you notice certain patterns across the board that students need to fix, conduct a minilesson before they apply or go back for a second round of ratiocination. For example, if you observe that students have a problem with initial words for starting a sentence, teach a minilesson on sentence connectors or transition words and phrases before asking students to draw a circle around each verb. The whole team then works together to correct.

Use Grammar Table Tents

Students need other tools to help with their writing. Distribute table tents with helpful charts such as shown in table 4.3. Tools like this help students become self-reliant (another subcategory of responsible decision making) and check their own work.

TABLE 4.3: Punctuation Marks and Their Usage

Punctuation Mark	Usage
Accent	Typically, only seen in words borrowed from another language, such as the Spanish word **melón**
Colon	Precedes an explanation or list
Comma	<ul><li>Separates items in a list</li><li>Separates clauses</li><li>Appears before and after an example or clarification</li><li>Appears before and after expressions such as **however**, **afterward**, **no doubt**, and so on</li></ul>
Ellipses	Continues a thought or indicates more content available in the original wording
Exclamation Mark	Appears only at the end of a sentence for emphasis
Hyphen	Serves to divide a word or connect two related adjectives

Parenthesis	Appears at the opening and closing of text included for clarification or elaboration
Period	Indicates the end of a sentence
Question Mark	Appears only at the end of a question
Quotation Marks	Appears at the beginning and end of a quote to indicate dialogue and when writing unfamiliar words
Semicolon	Indicates a longer pause than the comma but shorter than a period; separates items from a list that already has commas
Single Quotation Marks	Indicates a quote within a quote

Source: Calderón, Espino, & Slakk (2019).

Similarly, figure 4.4 shows several sentence starters suitable for table tents during this step of the collaborative writing process.

Initially	Moreover	In order to
Following that	Due to	So that implies
Additionally	Since	Thus
Subsequently	For this reason	As a result
Furthermore	Therefore	Finally

Source: Calderón, 2020.

FIGURE 4.4: Table tent for sentence starters.

*Visit **go.SolutionTree.com/EL** for a free reproducible version of this figure.*

STEP 4: REVISE USING THE CUT-AND-GROW STRATEGY

Students are usually reluctant to do multiple rewrites of their compositions. The *cut-and-grow* strategy allows students to make revisions without having to do a complete rewrite of their paper. After the rough draft is complete, students can look for places in their compositions where they might add more information or cite sources by using a sheet of colored paper on which to write the elaborated sentences and then tape the pieces together. This helps students immediately see how revisions improve their paper.

For example, they can add an introduction that catches the reader's attention. They can identify a sentence that requires evidence, supporting citations, or greater details.

Each team will need the following items.

- A sheet of colored paper
- Scissors
- Tape (or glue stick)
- Pencils

The steps for the cut-and-grow strategy are as follows.

1. Identify a sentence that should include more evidence, details, or support for a claim.
2. Carefully cut the composition just under the sentence where you want to add to the composition.
3. Write the new sentences on the colored paper. Glue the colored paper back into the draft.
4. Reread your enhanced compositions to the team and prepare to read to the whole class.

Figure 4.5 illustrates the steps and benefits for the cut-and-grow strategy.

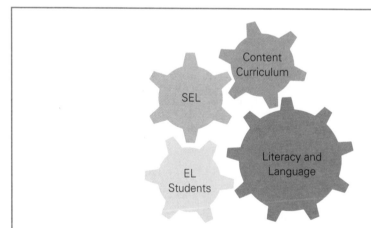

1. Identify a sentence that should include evidence, more details, or support for a claim.
2. Carefully cut the composition just under the sentence where you are going to add to the composition.
3. Write the new sentences on the colored paper. Glue the colored paper back into the draft.
4. Reread your enhanced compositions to the team and prepare to read to the whole class.

FIGURE 4.5: Steps for the cut-and-grow strategy.

Figure 4.6 shows two examples of the cut-and-grow strategy.

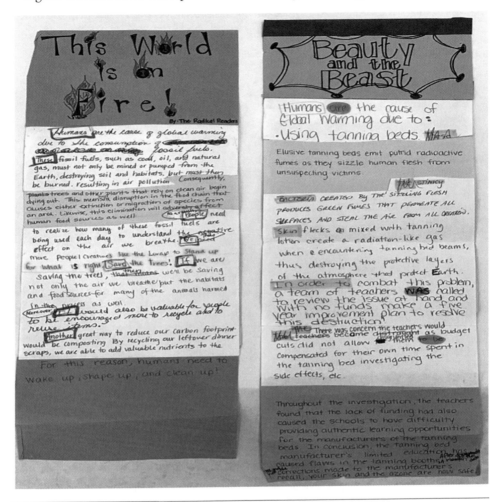

FIGURE 4.6: Examples of the cut-and-grow strategy.

STEP 5: WRITE INTRODUCTIONS AND CONCLUSIONS

Teach students the many kinds of leads and introductions by providing them with good models to learn from. Some different introductions or leads include those listed in figure 4.7.

Begin a composition with:		
Dialogue	Character	A flashback
Setting	Description	A problem
Action	A statistic	A historical perspective
Reaction	A quotation	

FIGURE 4.7: Ways to begin a composition.

*Visit **go.SolutionTree.com/EL** for a free reproducible version of this figure.*

Teach students the different ways to conclude or end a composition by again providing them with good models and examples to consider. Figure 4.8 lists methods students can use to write a powerful conclusion. For example, they can end a composition with a call to action or a quote.

Ways to end a composition with a powerful conclusion:		
Summary	Dialogue	Call back
Call to action	Clincher	Image
Surprise	Question	Quotation

FIGURE 4.8: Ways to end a composition.

*Visit **go.SolutionTree.com/EL** for a free reproducible version of this figure.*

Using a variety of mentor texts is a great way to teach both introductions and conclusions. Have students bring in books that they are reading and categorize the different types of leads and endings. Ask students to write several different leads or endings for their papers. In their writing group, peers can help English learners decide which lead or ending is the most effective.

STEP 6: SHARE AND FINALIZE

Once students are comfortable with their compositions, they read the composition aloud to their teams to practice (where necessary) fluency, prosody, pronunciation, pauses, and inflection, all of which help to teach grammar and sentence structures. When ready, student teams will read their paper to the whole class and get additional feedback on what others liked or would like to hear more of. It's important to keep this feedback session positive to sustain the motivation and excitement about writing.

Students need to know how well they did in identifying and coalescing important information into a meaningful learning experience. They need to know how well they accomplished their task, how well they used the learning strategies, and what they would do to improve next time. The feedback they get from sharing their work facilitates this, and they can further gauge their own performance using rubrics such as the one featured in figure 4.9.

On a scale of 1 (lowest) to 3 (highest), how well did you do? Which essential items did you use?			
Essentials for excellent writing	**Team**	**Myself**	**Next steps for improvement**
Difficult vocabulary words and in-text definitions			

Main ideas or arguments and related supporting evidence			
Headings, transitions, and other tier 2 words and phrases			
Illustrations, graphs, art, and other signposts			
Other difficult words (not discipline-specific vocabulary) and sentence construction			
Words for making inferences			
Words for drawing conclusions			

FIGURE 4.9: Performance rubric.

Visit **go.SolutionTree.com/EL** *for a free reproducible version of this figure.*

Encourage Collaborative Writing Online

Starting with the remote learning necessitated by the COVID-19 pandemic, teachers have found ways to facilitate team-based collaborative writing online through platforms like Zoom. Teachers share their screen to model writing, give instructions, and post key vocabulary for a reading. They further use breakout rooms to form collaborative writing teams, ensuring English learners are distributed among all teams. This gives English learners more exposure to and engagement with English even while learning online. Even so, encourage teams with a common first language to write in that language once in a while. Pride in one's home language is thus sustained with writing.

Each team in the Zoom breakout rooms discusses the content they just read before they begin to write a draft using the write-around strategy discussed earlier in this chapter, in the section Adopt the Collaborative Writing Process (page 113). It is easy for the teacher to jump in and listen to each team as they map out their draft. They do their write around by saying one sentence at a time and muting right after. The students write on the digital whiteboard. For the editing, they have ample discussions again using the ratiocination chart (see figure 4.3, page 117). Afterward, they can do a cut-and-grow strategy (see Step 4: Revise Using the Cut-and-Grow Strategy, page 119) online by actually cutting out a sentence or adding to sentences on the whiteboard or using a Google doc. In our experience, all students engage well with this process and are more excited to get it right, even when working online.

Continue Writing at Home

To continue building on the writing skills developed during team writing, teachers may find journaling at home to be one of the most effective tools to reinforce and support the ongoing process of English learners improving their writing. Journaling at home can also serve as an informal way for students to record their ideas and feelings after a particular team writing exercise or a teacher's minilesson. This could include writing about upcoming assignments or expectations in preparation for a trip, learning how to make a list of important tasks to do, or expressing themselves through a personal and creative outlet. As educator Charlie Merrow (n.d.) states, "Journaling has the added benefit of improving self-awareness and self-management, while providing a foundation for social awareness, relationship skills, and responsible decision making."

Writing in Elementary Grades

Writing in the elementary classroom is a very social process. Writing in the early years can start with a morning message using a shared writing approach. The teacher writes with the class on large chart paper or on an interactive board. The students work with a partner to compose the writing piece. Students rehearse the sentences with their partner. A great visual guide is for the students to say the sentence and touch each finger for each word they want in the sentence. Then they recite the sentence for the teacher to write on the board.

The teacher can choose various places in the piece for teaching points. Each student may have a copy of the text or use whiteboards to make the edits. The whole class can participate in ratiocination and edit for punctuation, capitalization, specificity, or other skills the teacher would like the students to practice.

As elementary students become more comfortable with writing, move them into journal writing and group writing, such as using the write-around strategy detailed in this chapter (page 115). Some English learners would benefit from having sentence starters for the write-around activity, which when paired with transition words help English learners structure their writing pieces. Eventually, as they become more confident in their writing, they will not have a need for sentence starters or other scaffolds.

When engaging with each other during the writing process, all students develop relationship skills such as communicating with others, practicing teamwork, collaborating, making decisions responsibly, and supporting each other.

Strategies for Administrators and Coaches

When observing writing instruction, administrators should look for students engaging with each other in small groups. Students collaborating with their peers should be visible as students are writing, talking, reading, and listening. Writing is an interactive process, and an observer should be able to see these interactions among students. Administrators should also look for writing that is authentic and meaningful to the students and not just an assignment but rather an engaging process. Administrators should also check for how teachers preteach skills in context through minilessons and modeling with think-alouds.

The following list details a few things coaches can do to support teachers.

- Help teachers create partnerships and groups.
- Make sure that groups are mixed in language proficiency and academic knowledge. Avoid placing all the multilingual learners and English learners in one team. They need language role models.
- Choose minilessons to teach based on student work.
- Help to find mentor texts as exemplars.
- Help create table tents to support student learning.
- Observe groups to see that all students are writing.

The following are things administrators and coaches can look for in a classroom.

- Students writing in small groups
- Authentic and meaningful writing
- Skills taught through minilessons
- Teacher modeling of writing processes

Support for Writing at Home

Writing at home can be an interactive process as well. Students should receive opportunities to write at home with real and authentic purposes. Families can support that writing by empowering students to engage in the writing process at home as well as engaging in the writing process with them.

As students write, parents help by offering sentence starters or by having the students rehearse each sentence before writing it. They can also go through the process with ratiocination (page 117) by editing for punctuation, spelling, capitalization, and specificity. Some examples of authentic writing are emails, recipes, cards, journals and diaries, and shopping lists.

When doing homework, students should do the writing and then have caregivers support them by helping them ratiocinate rather than correcting the work for them or telling them how to write it correctly the first time. Students need opportunities to write independently and then make corrections during ratiocination. Families may need to help with the ratiocination in the beginning, but the goal is for students to become intentional with this process. Figure 4.10 is an example summary to send to families to post at home.

Families and Caregivers

- Provide opportunities for authentic writing.
- Engage in the writing process with students.
- Provide sentence starters or rehearse before writing.
- Allow students to do their own writing and then provide support with ratiocination.
- The end goal is for students to be independent writers.

FIGURE 4.10: Summary for parents.

Questions From the Field

When we meet with teachers at workshops, they usually have important questions that we like to share with other teachers in brief responses, since the teachers are learning what we have presented in this book. Here are some that relate to writing for English learners and multilingual learners.

Do I need to wait for my English learners to develop listening and speaking abilities before they start writing?

Never keep English learners from writing. It will only hold them back. They can handle listening, speaking, reading, and writing simultaneously as long as they are supported by SEL motivational competencies and quality reading instruction. By the time they get to writing, the teacher has already pretaught vocabulary and English learners have read with peers, summarized (learning more vocabulary in the process), participated in class discussions, and formulated questions. They now have language and information to use in their writing.

How can I help my newcomers become good writers?

Start right away! Have them work in groups and complete activities like the write around. Give them table tents. You'll be grading the whole team product. Make sure you monitor their participation and track their language improvement.

I have several long-term English learners who have difficulty writing. How do I help them?

Have them draft a text-based composition with one or two peers, then teach them how to use ratiocination on a weekly basis. Once they practice editing for several weeks, introduce the cut-and-grow strategy to work on growing sentences.

What are some good materials on writing for English learners?

As of the time we are writing this book, there are none. No writing curriculum we are aware of has ever been written or tested for English learners. The best way to teach writing to them is for all core content teachers to implement effective instruction on writing that has been tested with English learners, which we have shared here with you.

Conclusion

As with vocabulary and reading, writing is just as much an academic exercise as it is social and emotional. Teaming strategies that focus on building relationships make writing much easier and attainable for English learners. Associating writing with social interactions with other students whom English learners have come to trust and have positive relationships with is essential for preparing English learners to write with greater ease and fluency. As with reading, English learners are also practicing the competencies of self-management, social awareness, responsible decision making, and relationship skills. Honoring and building on students' intrinsic motivation will lead to engagement and achievement. We have seen that with these writing strategies, English learners can associate classroom learning experiences with the opportunity to construct knowledge and co-create a writing product through a collaborative and cooperative process that is safe and motivating. Research shows that writing in the classroom can help students in setting and achieving goals, boosting memory and comprehension, improving communication skills, and providing organization practice, all of which leads to a reduction in stress (Pennebaker, 2004).

In summary, English learners need the following six items to become independent writers.

1. English learners need to work in interdependent teams writing a common text, using discourse and verbal interaction around the initial writing samples, and engaging in editing the final product.

2. English learners need examples of various writing genres and opportunities to discuss their individual attributes, purposes, and formats so that they can see and understand the differences.

3. An English learner's writing should be approached in a holistic fashion, from vocabulary to discourse to reading to writing.

4. English learners need writing divided into multiple dimensions to form procedures that are safe, simple, and structured.

5. English learners need a strategy for revising their writing to make their compositions better.

6. Writing should allow English learners to become aware of their own culture, language, social skills, emotional skills, and their connection to writing.

Tips for Reflection and Planning for Educators

- Evaluate the extent to which you require all students—especially the less experienced ones—to write extensively so that they can be comfortable writing.

- Create writing assignments that ask students to interpret and analyze across a wide variety of genres.

- Teach words, phrases, and sentence structures for each genre.

- Include reading in class for at least ten to fifteen minutes on the subject students are to write about.

- Select texts that are rigorous enough and at grade level and parse them for depth of reading.

- Provide opportunities for English learners to work in pairs, teams of four, or project-based teams for drafting, revising, editing, and peer feedback.

- Provide SEL and ExC-ELL discourse protocols, such as tier 2 connectors and phrases, norms for taking turns, interrupting, summarizing, elaborating, accepting multiple perspectives, and so on.

- Emphasize valuing the home language and culture by offering opportunities to write in that language.

- Provide reading materials that include culturally relevant selections and authentic literature such as newspapers.

- Provide assessment tools for students to use in peer reviews and self-reflections for continuous improvement.

- Employ multiple measures, including portfolios, to provide formative and summative evaluation.

Tips for a Whole-School Approach to Professional Development and Teacher Learning Communities

- Work for full commitment by everyone at the school to English learner success.

- Shift to an asset-based mindset to recognize how much English learners have learned at home during the school year.

- Build relationships with families and become partners with them.

- Create a policy for the use of home-language literacy in learning to read and becoming proficient readers.

- Teach parents ways to have ample discourse with their children, including vocabulary, songs, family histories, sayings, idioms, jokes, reading to them, and encouraging them to read.

- Strengthen cultural connections by having educators visit students' homes and learn about their cultures. Educators then connect what they find with instruction by providing students with books that represent them and the cultures educators observed in students' homes.

- Help teachers recognize where they and their colleagues need to grow their teaching strategies and diminish biases.

- Provide all teachers with professional development specific to writing for English learners.

- Give all teachers time to plan and integrate writing into existing lessons—especially lessons that haven't previously worked with English learners.

- Give all teachers access to SEL writing standards so they can explicitly teach and embed SEL competencies into writing lessons.

- Ensure everyone has clarity of what is equity and what is not: there is clarity of actions and conceptual clarity.

- Move all students in a similar direction to ensure grade-level reading for English learners.

To bring SEL, language, literacy, and content learning together in a way that makes a truly positive impact on English learners and their classmates, educators schoolwide need to work on students' disposition and skills. Therefore, how to accomplish this through a whole-school approach to professional learning is the topic of chapter 5.

Relationship Skills Applied to School-Classroom Communities

Key Term: Relationship Skills

Students with **relationship skills** have the ability to "establish and maintain healthy and supportive relationships and to effectively navigate settings with diverse individuals and groups," including the "capacities to communicate clearly, listen actively, cooperate, work collaboratively to problem solve and negotiate conflict constructively, navigate settings with differing social and cultural demands and opportunities, provide leadership, and seek or offer help when needed" (CASEL, n.d.d).

Emily was a high school English learner. She had been in the high school for a few years, was fluent in English, and successful in all of her high school classes; especially her art classes. Toward the end of the school year, many students participated in a volunteer school beautification project. She heard about the project but didn't really think much about it. Most of the English learners didn't really participate in the project, so she decided it just wasn't for her. That was until a teacher approached her.

The teacher said she recognized how great Emily's artwork was and wondered if she would be interested in an on-campus project. The project was to create some murals and paintings with inspirational quotes and sayings around the school.

Emily was intrigued by this and told the teacher she would get back to her.

Emily returned the next day with her project form signed and told the teacher she was very interested. The teacher connected her with several other students who were interested in the project as well. Emily met with the students, and together they planned out what they would be doing. They searched for quotes and pictures and planned for several murals around the school.

Emily went to each location and sketched what she wanted the murals to be. Then the group decided how much paint and brushes they needed. They broke up into smaller teams and began painting the murals. It took them a few weeks to finish, but the final products were amazing.

The teacher talked with Emily about the murals and Emily said, "This was the first time in four years I felt like I belonged." Emily worked with the other students and created several murals around the school. She was so proud of what they had accomplished.

Emily didn't feel included in her school until she got involved in the project. Working on a project with her peers gave her an opportunity to use her assets in a way that gave her a sense of belonging. A school with an integrated approach (literacy, language, and SEL) to learning, provides all students, including English learners, with space in which they can feel included and involved in their learning. Finding ways to build on a student's assets can help the student feel as if they contribute to the culture of the school. It provides them with a sense of belonging.

The COVID-19 pandemic that began in 2020 challenged students' relationship-building skills, especially as most schools resorted to virtual instruction. Students were away from peers for a long time, and the effects of that continue to be evident even after students returned to schools. According to a study from the Kaiser Family Foundation, more than 25 percent of high schoolers and more than 20 percent of children ages five to twelve reported the pandemic negatively affected their mental health (Panchal, Kamal, Cox, Garfield, & Chidambaram, 2021).

So how do educators repair what has been broken? How do schools create environments in which students feel a sense of belonging? What tools do students need to feel like they are able to contribute to the school and collaborate with others in the school? "The Evidence Base for How We Learn," a study by an alliance of scientists and scholars on improving student outcomes and authored by Stephanie M. Jones and Jennifer Kahn (2017), indicates that educators can shape contexts and experiences to positively affect children's social-emotional learning and their academic and life outcomes. Schools need to put more effort into meeting the social-emotional needs of their students. Relationship skills need to be modeled, retaught, and practiced repeatedly. Providing activities for students to engage with each other helps foster relationship skills. Helping students feel like they belong must be intentional and part of everything that schools do.

Our book has provided research, evidence, and strategies for content teachers to consider and implement procedures that will help to create a learning space in which all students can thrive. Providing literacy, language, and SEL instruction throughout all classes will help students have the tools they need to be active learners and the social-emotional competencies to engage with others. This chapter is different from the others in that it integrates those other chapters (SEL competencies and literacy components) with school and classroom strategies to create a culture and climate that encourage student engagement and belonging.

Relationship Skill Building for English Learners

Positive student relationships are fundamental to success. When students feel supported, they're more likely to engage in learning and have better academic outcomes (EdTrust & MDRC, 2021). Schools can provide those environments by being intentional about how teachers interact with students and providing opportunities for students to positively interact with each other.

There is a direct correlation between student relationships and student achievement. All students need a safe, warm, and welcoming environment to lay the foundation for positive relationships. English learners especially need supportive teacher and peer relationships to help develop English proficiency. When SEL is embedded into the curriculum (such as what is covered in this book), classrooms can be more welcoming and encouraging and provide opportunities for students to engage with each other. When students are in supportive learning environments and feel a sense of belonging, they are more engaged in their learning.

Creating positive and welcoming environments in which all students feel like they belong can be a challenge for schools. Even with best intentions, some students will still feel left out. Teachers should provide many opportunities for students to engage with each other. Too often, lessons lack student interaction and therefore missed opportunities for students to develop relationship skills. Taking time to incorporate those interactions will benefit all students, but especially English learners. When creating lessons, SEL should be part of the objectives. Teachers can create content, language, and SEL objectives to ensure that those opportunities are available for students.

Relationship skills can be part of the school climate and culture, but schools need to be mindful about implementation to ensure that all students have access. Educators should have supports in place to include all students. Those supports may include creating school norms, scaffolding, purposeful planning, and other intentional activities. Where do you start? How do you create a culture and climate that supports all learners? How do you ensure that students have the tools they need to be active learners? This chapter provides ways in which schools can be thoughtful about how to engage all students and support all relationship skills while integrating the literacy skills and SEL competencies highlighted throughout this book.

The Research on Relationship Skills and School-Classroom Communities

Research shows the importance of peer and adult relationships in a school setting, indicating a correlation between strong relationships and student achievement. A 2006 study by researchers Miranda J. Lubbers, Margaretha P.C. Van Der Werf, Tom A. B. Snijders, Bert P. M. Creemers, and Hans Kuyper affirms a relationship between peer acceptance and students' academic progress.

A 2019 study in the Cleveland Metropolitan School District showed all four domains of school climate (safety, teaching and learning, interpersonal relationships, and the institutional environment) were positively associated with a high English language-speaking proficiency level. In addition, English learner students who attended schools with higher student ratings of academic rigor and a supportive learning environment had higher English language arts performances. Students who attended schools with safer and more respectful climate ratings had higher listening proficiency levels (Garrett, Davis, & Eisner, 2019).

Research in human development establishes that social, emotional, and cognitive development are deeply intertwined and together are integral to academic learning and success (Jones & Kahn, 2017).

Relationship Skills Across All Content Areas

Social-emotional learning experts say that spending some classroom time explicitly teaching social-emotional skills is important, but what matters even more is effectively integrating the skills—such as time management, collaboration skills, and responsible decision making—into everything that students are learning in school and in after-school programs (Langreo, 2022). Teachers can embed SEL into all areas of the curriculum. SEL does not need to be an isolated subject or content. As stated in early chapters, SEL is inherent in literacy practices. As students engage in all four domains of language, they also engage in SEL practice. However, schools must be intentional about the SEL competencies they embed.

For example, when creating lessons or activities, after creating content objectives and language objectives, teachers can also create SEL objectives. When educators think about which SEL competencies each lesson will implement and let students practice, they will shift their thinking from just having final outcomes to the benefit of the processes.

When schools have initiatives or activities, SEL should be part of the discussion. How will the school include all students? How will teachers engage all students? How will they help support the SEL competencies through each activity or initiative being implemented?

Strategies to Build School and Classroom Culture

Creating schools and classrooms that encourage positive relationships takes planning. There are many strategies and routines that teachers can implement to create and support that environment. We have included a few of the strategies that effectively build and nurture a healthy classroom culture; they are as follows.

Make Working Agreements

To create a sense of community and ownership, students need to collaborate when creating class norms and agreements rather than adhering solely to teacher-created rules. Classroom-created norms created collaboratively with students are relevant and reflect what students desire in a working environment where they will be successful.

There are varying procedures teachers can use to help students create norms. One process that works effectively is to have students write on sticky notes one or two strategies, rules, or expectations that they believe would help create a positive working environment for all students to succeed. They should be written in positive language. For example, *"Use a quiet voice when working so that we can have a quiet work environment that supports all students."* After each student writes on their sticky notes, they give them to the teacher. For English learners, teachers can create *I need . . .* statements for what the student needs to have a successful working environment.

The teacher sorts the notes and places them in groups with other similar rules. Then the teacher shares the common groups and asks students to create category headings based on the similar groups of sticky notes.

After the categories are created (usually three to four total), the class creates an agreement based on the category. For example, comments about being kind, nice, respectful, and using active listening can go under the category of positive peer relationships. From that process, the class agreements are created. Publish them on chart paper and have every student in the class sign at the bottom.

Classroom-created working agreements help students feel they have voice and choice, empowering them to take ownership and responsibility for their class. The following are three steps to create classroom agreements together.

1. The teacher and students brainstorm some ideas as a class for what students need to make a positive working environment. Use *I need . . .* statements.

2. The teacher takes the statements and sorts them by themes.

3. The teacher posts the agreements as a poster and students sign the poster.

Start With Morning Meetings and Circle Time

Morning meetings in the classroom help students to connect at the very beginning of the day and are easy to implement online as well. Morning meetings are a time for students to come together in a circle and greet each other by name. Meetings should last from fifteen to twenty minutes. Stating student names provides a sense of belonging and a feeling of being included. Teachers should model the process for greetings and then have students practice. To facilitate this, teachers can provide sentence frames for students to say. For example, they can begin with something familiar, such as the following.

- "Good morning, _____. How are you today?"
- "I feel _____. How are you?"

Subsequently, educators can ask how students are feeling. To aid English learners, they can preteach tier 2 feeling words using the seven-step method we introduced in chapter 1 for preteaching vocabulary (page 27). Teachers can also place charts like the one shown in figure 5.1 around the room with pictures so that students can be specific about how they are feeling.

How are you feeling today?				
Happy 😃	Sad 😖	Tired 😴	Worried 🙁	Excited 🤗
Motivated 😉	Grumpy 😠	Nervous 😟	Fantastic 😄	Joyful 😌
Calm 🙂	Just OK 🙂	Peaceful 😇	Fearful 😳	Marvelous 😁

FIGURE 5.1: Emotional check-in chart.

*Visit **go.SolutionTree.com/EL** for a free reproducible version of this figure.*

Greeting each other by name helps students to feel seen and valued. For many students, including your English learners, this meeting may be the first time someone greeted them by name that day. It also helps students learn each other's names, and this process may spill into other areas such as the hallway, other classes, and in the community. If students need help learning each other's names, consider using name tags, as pictured in figure 5.2 (page 138).

FIGURE 5.2: Name tag.

Another component of morning meeting time might be time for students to share stories or items, like show and tell. Teachers may model the expectations for sharing time. Providing sentence frames for English learners, like the ones sampled in figure 5.3, will help them feel more comfortable with sharing.

I want to share _____ .	This is important to me because _____ .
I brought this today because _____ .	This is my _____ .
_____ is meaningful to me because _____ .	_____ is my favorite because _____ .

FIGURE 5.3: Sharing sentence frames.

*Visit **go.SolutionTree.com/EL** for a free reproducible version of this figure.*

As students use these frames in the circle, their peers ask clarifying questions about the story or objects. The teacher models the process with appropriate types of questions to ask and preteaches tier 2 words that may be in the questions. Figure 5.4 lists possible items and story questions teachers can post in the classroom as a reminder to students of questions they can ask.

Where did you get that?	Who was with you in your story?
How did you feel in your story?	Why was this important to you?
Where were you?	How did you feel when you got that item?

FIGURE 5.4: Clarifying questions.

*Visit **go.SolutionTree.com/EL** for a free reproducible version of this figure.*

Sharing stories or items is an important part of learning and growth. Sharing, the second component of a morning meeting, plays an important role in building a positive classroom community. Just as importantly, sharing offers ample opportunities to practice and reinforce the speaking, listening, and thinking skills that are so crucial to school success (Kriete & Davis, 2014). Sharing provides a place for students to be vulnerable and for other students to connect and provide support for their peers. Students may tell stories about something great that happened to them recently or stories about a disappointment. Hearing the stories of others helps students to develop empathy. It also helps students to understand other perspectives and breaks down some of the barriers of the unknown. The latter is especially significant, as unknowns can cause fear and be the root cause for anger, bullying, and so on. Sharing is an important time for students to get to know each other, celebrate, anticipate, and mourn together.

Another component of morning meetings might be team building or something done as a group. This collaborative activity might be a game, a song, a book, role plays, or a poem. If the class reads something together, the teacher parses the piece that the students will read and selects tier 2 words to preteach. The selected reading can be a familiar poem or song lyrics that students can read aloud together or a new text that the teacher will lead the class through. Some text examples are a seasonal poem or song or a content area passage. The teacher may lead the class through a shared reading experience or read to the class during this time. Discovering a character together as a class can also build connections. Reciting a poem or song together can develop unity. If the teacher chooses a game or challenge, it helps foster relationship skills. The teacher could also lead students through a mindfulness practice or body movement practice (Kriete & Davis, 2014).

Use Written Messages

Written messages are ideas, goals, or rules you write together with the class. The final part of the morning meeting is the written message. Some ideas for the written message are *morning message, working agreements*, or *class goals*. For example, if the class is struggling with cell phone use or talking during independent work time, the class can work on and write out agreements during this time. The agreement will help the students work together with the end goal in mind or everyone being successful at what they are doing. The following are some morning message ideas for teams of students or the whole class.

- **Letter to the class:** The teacher could write the morning message to the class. For example, the teacher could write about something students will be learning or directions for getting their field trip forms completed.

- **Letter to another class, teacher, principal, or custodian:** For example, the class could write a thank you letter to the custodian for making their classroom look clean.

- **Summary of goals or objectives for the day:** For example, the class could write about subject goals or SEL goals for the day.

- **Working agreements:** The class could create working agreements. If students need to work on something independently, the norms could focus on creating a quiet working environment. If the class had group work, students could create norms for engaging with their groups.

- **A summary of a book or story read during morning meeting:** The class could write a summary of a book or article they are reading.

- **A summary of stories told by students during sharing time:** The class could practice summarizing by writing a summary of the story that a class member told during meeting time.

Morning meetings provide a starting place for the day. They help English learners and their peers become grounded and feel connected with their teacher and peers. Morning meetings lay the foundation for the day and help set the intentions for the day (Kriete & Davis, 2014).

Make School Activities Accessible to All

All students want to feel like they belong, but English learners especially may sometimes feel disconnected from the school. For example, they may not understand traditional activities that are part of the school culture. We can't assume that all students listen to the morning news or read the newsletter. Schools need to develop plans to ensure that all students have access to things that take place in the school and that they all understand the activities throughout the school day.

In high schools, there are so many things going on before, during, and after school. There are extracurricular activities, sports, spirit days, pep rallies, clubs, and many other traditional activities that take place. Newcomers and English learners may not understand what those things are and so may not participate. School staff might assume that these students are not interested, when in fact, had they received more information, they may want to participate.

For example, homecoming is an exciting time of year for high schoolers. There are spirit days, parades, decorating, dances, pep rallies, and football games. English learners may have never heard of the homecoming traditions of the United States before. To help them understand, teachers can write a passage about each of the homecoming activities. Then the teacher can preteach the vocabulary related to homecoming using the seven-step method (see page 27 in chapter 1). The students can partner read the passage and summarize each section. They can talk about what they learned and write about what things they would like to know more about or what things they would like to participate in.

This activity can help English learners to feel included. It can also encourage relationship skills because now students will understand events taking place in the school, and they may be more inclined to participate. The following are some topics to write about.

- Homecoming
- Prom
- Field day
- Pep rally
- Spirit week
- Graduation
- Field trips
- Sports
- Awards ceremony
- Talent show
- School play or musical

Being a part of team, participating in a club, or volunteering can all be opportunities for students to learn SEL competencies in school, especially relationship skills. Packaged SEL programs are effective, but making SEL part of every aspect of the school is where there will be the most impact (Cohen et al., 2021).

Trying different sports or activities gives students opportunities to find something they enjoy and self-determine their identity. However, sometimes English learners may not have access to those activities. Auditions, tryouts, and club invitations are usually announced on the morning news, on the website, or on fliers that hang in areas of the school. English learners can miss such announcements, so being intentional about talking about those things in classes can help them to become more aware of opportunities in the school. After the announcements, teachers should have the students summarize what was said to their partner and ask clarifying questions to get more information. The following are the steps to summarize the morning announcements.

1. Provide students with a written copy of the announcements.

2. Preteach any tier 2 vocabulary words.

3. Have students listen to the announcements and follow along with the copy.

4. Have students partner read the announcements and summarize.

5. Have students ask clarifying questions.

6. Students who are interested in any of the activities ask the teacher how to get the resources and the teacher gets the student connected to those resources.

Registering for sports, in particular, can be complicated. Students need to complete forms, show proof of health insurance, get a physical or vaccinations, and need transportation to get home from practices or games. Again, schools need to ensure all students have access to those activities and provide resources to help. A great literacy lesson would be to go over applications for sports or clubs. The teacher parses the application and looks for tier 2 and 3 words to preteach. Then the students partner with each other to read the application and summarize each part of the application. The teacher can also introduce text features for team schedules, team websites, and more.

Establish Norms of Engagement With Students and Families

In addition to having classroom norms in the form of working agreements (page 136), encouraging positive relationships in the school, faculty, and staff also requires modeling those expectations. Creating schoolwide norms for staff engagement with students can help make that modeling intentional and create a warm and welcoming climate.

By creating norms for engaging with students and families, the staff will be intentional about connecting with them. This practice not only models positive interactions but also shows students that teachers see, hear, and value them. This intentional and reflective process will help staff ensure that all students are being included.

Schools can use school climate surveys for ideas of areas that they need to address. If students and families report that communication is lacking, the school norms can focus on communication that year. If students say they don't feel seen or heard, then norms can focus on listening or student voice and choice. The norms can change year to year and staff can reflect on them quarterly. This process can also be used with making classroom norms.

The following is a list of steps for creating school norms for engagement with students.

1. Staff or faculty members write their answers to the following prompt: The most positive and supportive process I had with a student was _____ because _____ .

2. Sort the notes into common themes and attach them to large pieces of chart paper.

3. Staff or faculty does a gallery walk to view each poster, observes the themes on each, and creates a *We will . . .* statement. For example, *We will call each student by name and pronounce it correctly when we see that student in and outside of the classroom.*

4. From those statements, the staff or faculty collaborates to create a list of *We will . . .* statements to use as norms for engaging with students.

Figure 5.5 offers examples of a few norms of engagement with students.

- We will actively listen to students when they talk to us.
- We will praise students with positive comments through notes, public praise, and phone calls home.
- We will communicate with families through emails, the website, and phone calls home.
- We will spend the beginning of each class greeting each student and checking in with how they are doing.
- We will spend time in our classes allowing students to talk about how things are going in school and in life.
- We will offer voice and choice at least once during a lesson.
- We will send at least one positive email home a day.

FIGURE 5.5: Sample norms of engagement with students.

Build Collective Efficacy for All Through Staff Development

Just as we have collective efficacy and peer relationships as goals for English learners and all students, we also need to think about collective efficacy for educators. Schools and teachers are still feeling the effects of the COVID-19 pandemic. These include shortages of teaching staff and having to stand in for vacant staff positions, reduced time for professional learning with colleagues, concern over missing students or recurring absenteeism, a rise in school violence, hybrid instruction requiring double planning, and many other sources of uncertainty and unexpected challenges.

Educator's self-efficacy manifests in their collective belief that they can learn new ways of instructing newcomers. Deriving his findings from the work of education researcher Kenneth Leithwood (2006), Chase Mielke (2021), an award-winning educator and speaker, links high levels of teacher self-efficacy to the following.

- Increased persistence and patience when helping struggling students learn
- Greater willingness to try new approaches
- Increased parental involvement in school
- Higher levels of student achievement across diverse demographics
- Increased job satisfaction
- Lower levels of burnout, exhaustion, and apathy

These characteristics are fitting for teachers of newcomers. Working with newcomers means persistence, patience, and a willingness to try new approaches, such as those we describe in this book. It also means increasing engagement with their multilingual families. At the same time, the teacher's job satisfaction and well-being increase when observing the immediate growth in the newcomer's language, literacy, and content knowledge.

For teachers to develop this level of collective self-efficacy for newcomers, the district and school leadership must provide quality professional development and support systems where collegiality materializes. There are many studies that direct us to implement evidence-based professional learning and follow-up teacher support systems. In the 1980s, Bruce Joyce and Beverly Showers (1988), whose research spans decades, introduced the components of effective professional learning and coaching.

They wrote and presented the following components on what professional learning workshops should include.

1. Theory and research on a given instructional model
2. Modeling or demonstrations of the strategies
3. Practice of strategies by the participants at the workshop and feedback by the facilitators
4. Follow-up coaching to ensure transfer from training

Figure 5.6 illustrates a structure to apply to your professional learning efforts.

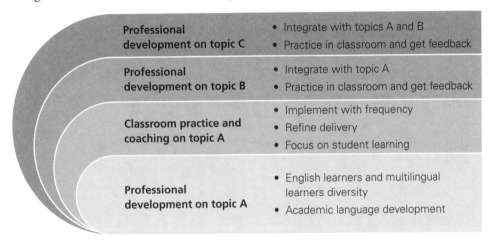

FIGURE 5.6: Professional learning.

These components were replicated in a professional learning study with elementary general education teachers with English learners. Fifty teachers of English learners from five school districts in Southern California attended a one-week institute on instructional strategies for English learners. After the week of professional learning, the teachers were randomly assigned to either receive coaching or no coaching. Pre- and postdata on teachers and their English learners demonstrate the value of coaching as compared to English learners and their teachers who did not receive coaching (Calderón, 2007b). Eighty percent of the coached teachers implemented the instructional strategies with frequency and fidelity as recommended over two years. They developed a sense of self-efficacy in one year, and after two years, they became exceptional teachers. Many became trainers and coaches themselves.

The other 20 percent of coached teachers took two years to reach the same level of efficacy as their colleagues. Those that took two years reported that they were influenced by their colleagues who were implementing the strategies and seeing great results with English learners. They saw how English learners were more confident and eager to learn compared to English learners they had in years before. This boosted teacher effectiveness during the second year. From this, we learned that some teachers readily adopt and adapt the instruction in one year while others need more time (Calderón, 1984; Calderón & Montenegro, 2021).

Based on these and other studies from mainstream researchers, we built and refined a whole-school professional learning model that consists of the following features.

1. Teachers and administrators attend an initial twelve-hour institute to learn the basics of the following.

   a. Understanding the diversity of multilingual learners

   b. Adopting a strengths-based approach to supporting multilingual learners and newcomers in particular

   c. Teaching academic language, vocabulary, and discourse

   d. Teaching basic reading and reading comprehension

   e. Teaching drafting, editing, revising, and creative publications

   f. Developing assessments for English learners

2. Teachers and administrators do the following follow-up coaching sessions.

   a. Begin with expert coaching by the institute facilitators.

   b. Site-based coaches and administrators shadow the expert coaches and attend a session on how to use the observation protocol, give feedback, and mutually plan next steps.

   c. Coaches continue to work with teachers who are reluctant to be observed by: (1) co-planning a lesson, (2) reviewing or giving feedback on a lesson, (3) coaching teachers' rehearsal of what they plan to say to their students for a given strategy, and (4) co-teaching a lesson.

   d. Besides one-on-one coaching, coaches conduct a small- or large-group review of strategies.

   e. Coaches sustain coaching sessions throughout the school year.

How Administrators and Coaches Can Support Teachers

Receiving effective communication with feedback from administrators and coaches is essential for the teacher's professional success. Feedback can make or break a relationship, both between educators and between educators and students. Learning occurs within relationships. The healthier the relationship, the more learning takes place (Knight, 2021). Teaching newcomers or any English learners is probably new to the coach and the teacher. Thus, both need tools and preparation to make it work. The first step is to ensure that the coaches attend with teachers all professional learning sessions that impact English learner instruction.

After engaging in professional learning on integrating language, literacy, SEL, and content, schedule a session for teachers and coaches on how to prepare for coaching and teaching. This session's purpose is to include communication protocols and a review of the observation protocol that mirrors the twelve components for English learner instruction (see chapter 2, page 43). The session also covers how to give productive feedback and how to help teachers plan the growth path for their English learners. Participants discuss the before, during, and after coaching routines at the session.

Before the observation, the teacher takes the lead by informing the coach what strategy they will be working on during the observation—such as the seven-step method for preteaching vocabulary (page 27), partner reading with summarization (page 59), or a cooperative learning strategy—as itemized on the protocol. The focus of the observation can be on the teacher or on the English learners.

This type of preobservation briefing helps the coach and teacher determine the data to collect, such as teacher delivery, student engagement, and student discourse patterns. After the observation, the coach presents the data and listens, asks questions, and determines the next steps for the teacher and their English learners.

Support for Relationship Skills at Home

When schools went to remote learning during the COVID-19 pandemic, many students lost contact with schools. Lack of access to the internet, the need to support their families, and other issues prevented many students from participating in their classes.

As the 2020–2021 school year began, schools implemented many programs to try to engage those students. Sending voicemail and written messages, providing computers with internet service, providing food, and conducting home visits helped to bridge those gaps. As educators, we learned many different strategies from that year to help involve the families in student learning.

Communication with student families and caregivers needs to be consistent and intentional. Sending messages in home languages and providing links for resources and access can help ensure that families of English learners stay informed. Hosting meetings to instruct families and caregivers how to access grades, lesson platforms, and sports information can also help enhance communication efforts.

Involving families and caregivers in student goal setting and instruction can help enhance students' learning experience. Newcomer families need support to ease the transition to a new country and new school. Many parts of the U.S. education system are different than that of other countries. We cannot assume that families and caregivers know how schools operate in the United States. Having welcome centers can help provide that information and support.

Families need SEL support too. Schools need to create regular opportunities for families and caregivers to connect with the schools and build relationships. If families only get calls when something is not going well, that connection is not helpful. Families need to hear from schools when things are going well. Families need to be invited to community events, sporting events, and activities. Quick emails or phone calls can help show families that we care about their children.

Questions From the Field

Creating a shift in school climate and culture to support all leaners can be challenging but is possible. Many questions may arise on how to create those environments. The following are some common questions that schools may ask when working toward that shift.

How can I create opportunities for English learners to feel like they belong?

Help them build relationships with opportunities to meet and mingle with classmates. Provide discourse frames for them to use.

My high school English learners do not feel included in the school culture. How do we make our school more inclusive?

Use the cooperative learning strategies in chapter 3 (page 82). Convey care and concern for your English learners that extend beyond the classroom, such as in the vignette that opens this chapter.

I understand the need to integrate SEL with language, literacy, and my content area, but how do I develop efficacy?

Ask your school to provide a comprehensive, yearlong professional learning program that includes the twelve components of effective instruction for English learners (page 43). Also participate in coaching, taking the lead in determining which of the twelve components you want to work on and why.

My English language co-teacher and I need time to build our relationship and plan how our lessons can do more for our newcomers, who are students with interrupted formal education. How can we find this time?

Ask your administration to allocate planning time together and to set up teacher learning communities or collaborative teams where several teachers can exchange ideas.

As a principal, I have been told to rebuild educator agency and relationships in our school. Where do I begin?

Begin by providing at least three days of professional development on English learner instruction and additional days throughout the year. Establish a coaching program for all teachers and consider making teacher learning communities or collaborative teams a part of this program. Finally, track the progress of all English learners and celebrate!

Conclusion

There's an increase of violence in schools. Students are feeling like they don't belong. They are feeling stressed and anxious. Teachers are facing burnout and leaving the industry. Principals are struggling with the difficulties of making hard decisions. Families are losing trust in schools and fear for their children. It behooves the school leadership to implement SEL schoolwide for students and adults. Many of the issues can be ameliorated with an intentional focus on SEL. These practices will create a positive, engaging, and welcoming space for English learners to grow and flourish. The following are ten takeaways from this chapter.

1. Due to increased violence in schools, it behooves the school leadership to study and implement SEL schoolwide for students and adults.

2. Students need to be invited to activities within the school to create a sense of belonging.

3. Teachers are facing burnout and are leaving the industry.

4. Teachers need time out to plan their lessons since they are doing double duty due to staffing shortages and hybrid teaching.

5. With so many newcomers arriving, teachers now need to retool.

6. Principals are also burning out due to increasingly difficult decisions.

7. All students are stressed and anxious due to having to wear masks, being at risk for COVID, peer bullying, and the upsurge of violence in schools.

8. Without tools and training, coaches will struggle to be successful.

9. Families are losing trust in schools and fear for their children, so schools need to be intentional about rebuilding that trust.

10. All of the issues listed here can be ameliorated with an intentional focus on SEL as the whole school practices new instruction for English learners.

In summary, English learners need the following six items to build relationship skills and thrive in school-classroom communities.

1. Opportunities to work with other students in positive ways

2. Classrooms that create a sense of belonging and community

3. Schools that create a warm, welcoming, and affirming culture

4. Intentional invitations to increase access to school activities with complementary teaching and discussion of school activities and traditions

5. Personal and regular invitations for families to engage in their child's academic career

6. Effective professional learning for teachers, coaches, and administrators

The COVID-19 pandemic helped us to see the inequities of the past and the strengths possible during the resulting education situations. We can now map out next educational endeavors that continue to promote success for multilingual and English learners. By promoting SEL throughout the school day, all students will feel valued and seen. We can provide a space where English learners can be successful. Best wishes to you and your English learners!

Tips for Reflection and Planning for Administrators

- As time-consuming as it might seem, surveys on relationships will shed light on what is going well and what needs to improve.

- Encourage all core content teachers to strive to build relationships with newcomers and other English learners.

- Work to intentionally promote well-being and high expectations in relationships with English learners.

- Develop a scale of 1 to 5, with 1 being *needs improvement* and 5 being *excellent* to rate relationships between English learners and mainstream students.

- Determine what your school has in place to build relationships for English learners in school and after-school activities.

- Plan lessons to include cooperative learning strategies in all classrooms to build relationships and give English learners opportunities to practice the language of building relationships.

- Develop ways for your school to build stronger relationships with the families of English learners.

Tips for a Whole-School Approach to Professional Development and Teacher Learning Communities

- Seek out comprehensive professional learning on evidence-based instruction for English learners that provides theory, research, modeling, demonstrations, practice, and feedback at each workshop.

- Select comprehensive professional development that includes instruction on communicating clearly, listening actively, cooperating, working collaboratively to problem solve and negotiate conflict constructively, navigating settings with differing social and cultural demands and opportunities, providing leadership, and seeking or offering help when needed for all students and adults.

- Evaluate whether the SEL program is promoting equity and student and school adjustment.

- Require that the whole school (teachers, coaches, and administration) participates in the professional development on newcomers and English learner instruction.

- See that all core content teachers participate in follow-up coaching after the professional development.

- Provide coaches and teachers with a professional learning session on coaching in classrooms with English learners.

- Establish teacher learning communities for teachers to further study the implementation of new teaching approaches.

- Collect implementation data; analyze and use to adjust school procedures.

References and Resources

AAP News. (2021, October 19). *AAP, AACAP, CHA declare national emergency in children's mental health.* Accessed at https://publications.aap.org/aapnews /news/17718 on March 17, 2022.

August, D., & Calderón, M. (2006). Teacher beliefs and professional development. In D. August & T. Shanahan (Eds.), *Developing literacy in second-language learners: Report of the National Literacy Panel on Language-Minority Children and Youth* (pp. 555–580). Mahwah, NJ: Lawrence Erlbaum Associates.

August, D., Calderón, M., & Carlo, M. (2002). *Transfer of skills from Spanish to English: A study of young learners* [Technical report]. Washington, DC: Center for Applied Linguistics.

August, D., Carlo, M., Calderón, M., & Proctor, P. (2005, Spring). Development of literacy in Spanish-speaking English-language learners: Findings from a longitudinal study of elementary school children. *The International Dyslexia Association, 31*(2), 17–19.

August, D., & Shanahan, T. (Eds.). (2006). *Developing literacy in second language learners: Report of the National Literacy Panel on Language Minority Children and Youth.* Mahwah, NJ: Lawrence Erlbaum Associates.

Beck, I. L., & McKeown, M. G. (1991). Conditions of vocabulary acquisition. In R. Barr, M. L. Kamil, P. B. Mosenthal, & P. D. Pearson (Eds.), *Handbook of reading research* (Vol. 2, pp. 787–814). White Plains, NY: Longman.

Beck, I. L., McKeown, M. G., & Kucan, L. (2002). *Bringing words to life: Robust vocabulary instruction.* New York: Guilford Press.

Beck, I. L., McKeown, M. G., & Kucan, L. (2005). Choosing words to teach. In E. H. Hiebert & M. L. Kamil (Eds.), *Teaching and learning vocabulary: Bringing research to practice* (pp. 207–222). Mahwah, NJ: Lawrence Erlbaum Associates.

Berk, L. E. (2013). *Child development* (9th ed.). London: Pearson.

Biancarosa, G., & Snow, C. E. (2006). *Reading next: A vision for action and research in middle and high school literacy.* Washington, DC: Alliance for Excellent Education.

Bobek, B. L., Schnieders, J. Z., Moore, R., Way, J. D., & Burrus, J. (2021). *School counselors' perspectives on students' social/emotional development: Highlights and recommendations.* Accessed at https://www.act.org/content/dam/act/unsecured/documents/2021/School-Counselor-Perspectives-on-Student-Social-Emotional-Development-Brief.pdf on October 31, 2022.

Calderón, M. E. (1984). *Training bilingual trainers: A quantitative and ethnographic study of coaching and its impact on the transfer of training* [Unpublished doctoral dissertation]. Claremont Graduate School and San Diego State University.

Calderón, M. E. (2007a). *RIGOR! Reading instructional goals for older readers.* New York: Benchmark Education.

Calderón, M. E. (2007b). *Teaching reading to English language learners, grades 6–12: A framework for improving achievement in the content areas.* Thousand Oaks, CA: Corwin.

Calderón, M. E. (2011). *Teaching reading and comprehension to English learners, K–5.* Bloomington, IN: Solution Tree Press.

Calderón, M. E. (Ed.) (2012). *Breaking through: Effective instruction and assessment for reaching English learners.* Bloomington, IN: Solution Tree Press.

Calderón, M. E. (2020). Getting newcomers into the academic flow. *Educational Leadership, 77*(4), 68–73.

Calderón, M. E., August, D., Slavin, A., Cheung, A., Duran, D., & Madden, N. (2005). Bringing words to life in classrooms with English language learners. In E. H. Hiebert & M. L. Kamil (Eds.)., *Teaching and learning vocabulary: Bringing research to practice* (pp. 115–136). Mahwah, NJ: Lawrence Erlbaum Associates.

Calderón, M. E., & Carreón, A. (2018). Teaching vocabulary before, during and after reading. In L. Gerena & K. M. Reynolds (Eds.), *The TESOL encyclopedia of English language teaching* (pp. 1–7). New York: Wiley.

Calderón, M. E., Espino, G., & Slakk, S. (2019). *Integrando lenguaje, lectura, escritura y contenidos en español e inglés (Integrating language, reading, writing and content in English and in Spanish).* El Monte, CA: Velázquez Press.

Calderón, M. E., Hertz-Lazarowitz, R., & Slavin, R. (1998). Effects of bilingual cooperative integrated reading and composition on students making the transition from Spanish to English reading. *The Elementary School Journal, 99*(2). Accessed at www.journals.uchicago.edu/doi/abs/10.1086/461920 on March 17, 2022.

Calderón, M. E., & Minaya-Rowe, L. (2003). *Designing and implementing two-way bilingual programs: A step-by-step guide for administrators, teachers, and parents.* Thousand Oaks, CA: Corwin.

Calderón M. E., & Minaya-Rowe, L. (2011). *Preventing long-term ELs: Transforming schools to meet core standards.* Thousand Oaks, CA: Corwin.

Calderón M. E., & Montenegro, H. (2021). *Empowering long-term ELs with social-emotional learning, language, and literacy.* El Monte, CA: Velázquez Press.

Calderón, M. E., & Slakk, S. (2017). *Promises fulfilled: A leader's guide for supporting English learners.* Bloomington, IN: Solution Tree Press.

Calderón, M. E., & Slakk, S. (2018). *Teaching reading to English learners, grades 6–12: A framework for improving achievement in the content areas* (2nd ed.). Thousand Oaks, CA: Corwin.

Calderón, M. E., & Slakk, S. (2019). *Success with multicultural newcomers and English learners: Proven practices for school leadership teams.* Alexandria, VA: ASCD.

Calderón, M. E., & Slakk, S. (2020a, August). From language to language, literacy, and content: Breaking down the wall, one essential shift at a time. *Language Magazine*, p. 33–35.

Calderón, M. E., & Slakk, S. (2020b). From language to language, literacy, and content. In Calderón, M. E., Dove, M., Fenner, D. S., Gottlieb, M., Honigsfeld, A., Singer T. W., et al. (Eds.), *Breaking down the wall: Essential shifts for English learners' success* (pp. 111–134). Thousand Oaks, CA: Corwin.

Calderón, M. E., Slavin, R. E., & Sánchez, M. (2011). Effective instruction for English language learners. *The Future of Children, 21*(1), 103–128.

Calderón, M.E., & Tartaglia, L. (2020, May 13). *Core-content teachers: You can provide good distance learning for English learners* [Blog post]. Accessed at https://www.ascd.org/blogs/core-content-teachers-you-can-provide-good -distance-learning-for-english-learners on August 2, 2022.

Calderón, M. E., Trejo, M. N., & Montenegro, H. (2016). *Literacy strategies for English learners in core content secondary classrooms.* Bloomington, IN: Solution Tree Press.

Calderón, M. E., Trower, L. M., Tartaglia, L. M., & Montenegro, H. (2022). *Expediting comprehension for English learners (ExC-ELL) teachers manual* (9th ed.). Washington, DC: Margarita Calderón & Associates, Inc.

Carlo, M. S., August, D., & Snow, C. E. (2005). Sustained vocabulary-learning strategy instruction for English language learners. In E. H. Hiebert & M. L. Kamil (Eds.), *Teaching and learning vocabulary: Bringing research to practice* (pp. 137–154). Mahwah, NJ: Lawrence Erlbaum Associates.

Collaborative for Academic, Social, and Emotional Learning. (n.d.a). *CASEL program guide.* Accessed at https://pg.casel.org/ on August 2, 2022.

Collaborative for Academic, Social, and Emotional Learning. (n.d.b). *Fundamentals of the SEL framework.* Accessed at https://casel.org /fundamentals-of-sel on May 2, 2022.

Collaborative for Academic, Social, and Emotional Learning. (n.d.c). *What is social and emotional learning?* Accessed at https://drc.casel .org/what-is-sel on May 4, 2022.

Collaborative for Academic, Social, and Emotional Learning. (n.d.d). *What is the CASEL framework?* Accessed at https://casel.org/fundamentals-of-sel /what-is-the-casel-framework/#the-casel-5 on May 2, 2022.

Chall, J. S. (1996). American reading achievement: Should we worry? *Research in the Teaching of English, 30*(3), 303–310.

Cohen, R. K., Opatosky, D. K., Savage, J., Stevens, S. O., & Darrah, E. P. (2021). *The metacognitive student: How to teach academic, social, and emotional intelligence in every content area.* Bloomington, IN: Solution Tree Press.

Collier, V. P., & Thomas, W. P. (2004). The astounding effectiveness of dual language education for all. *NABE Journal of Research and Practice, 2*(1), 1–20.

Committee for Children. (2022). *What is social-emotional learning?* Accessed at https://www.cfchildren.org/what-is-social-emotional-learning/ on August 2, 2022.

Cunningham, A. E., & Stanovich, K. E. (1998). The impact of print exposure on word recognition. In J. L. Metsala & L. C. Ehri (Eds.), *Word recognition in beginning literacy* (pp. 235–262). Mahwah, NJ: Lawrence Erlbaum Associates.

Dalton, S. S. (1998). *Pedagogy matters: Standards for effective teaching practice.* Accessed at https://escholarship.org/uc/item/6d75h0fz on August 2, 2022.

Darling-Hammond, L., & Bransford, J. (Eds.). (2005). *Preparing teachers for a changing world: What teachers should learn and be able to do.* San Francisco: Jossey-Bass.

Dweck, C. S. (2017). *Mindset: Changing the way you think to fulfil your potential* (Updated ed.). New York: Ballantine Books.

Echevarría, J., Vogt, M., & Short, D. J. (2008). *Making content comprehensible for English learners: The SIOP model.* New York: Pearson.

EdTrust & MDRC. (2021, March 17). *Expanded learning time.* Accessed at https://edtrust.org/resource/expanded-learning-time/ on August 2, 2022.

Farstrup, A. E., & Samuels, S. J. (2002). Reading fluency: Its development and assessment. In A. E. Farstrup & S. J. Samuel (Eds.), *What research has to say about reading instruction* (3rd ed, pp. 166–183). Newark, DE: International Reading Association.

Garrett, R., Davis, E., & Eisner, R. (2019, June). Student and school characteristics associated with academic performance and English language proficiency among English learner students in grades 3–8 in the Cleveland Metropolitan School District. Accessed at https://files.eric.ed.gov/fulltext/ED595192.pdf on August 2, 2022.

Genesee, F., Lindholm-Leary, K., Saunders, W., & Christian, D. (2006). *Educating English language learners: A synthesis of research evidence.* New York: Cambridge University Press.

Graham, S., & Perin, D. (2007). *Writing next: Effective strategies to improve writing of adolescents in middle and high schools.* Washington, DC: Alliance for Excellent Education.

Graham, S., & Sandmel, K. (2011). The process writing approach: A meta-analysis. *The Journal of Educational Research, 104*(6), 396–407.

Graves, M. F., & Sales, G. C. (2013). *Teaching 50,000 words: Meeting and exceeding the Common Core State Standards for vocabulary.* Accessed at www.literacyworldwide.org/docs/default-source/member-benefits /e-ssentials/ila-e-ssentials-8035.pdf on March 17, 2022.

Hart, B., & Risley, T. R. (1995). *Meaningful differences in the everyday experience of young American children.* Baltimore: Brookes Publishing.

Hattie, J. (2012). *Visible learning for teachers: Maximizing impact on learning.* New York: Routledge.

Hiebert, E. H., & Kamil, M. L. (Eds.). (2005). *Teaching and learning vocabulary: Bringing research to practice.* Mahwah, NJ: Lawrence Erlbaum Associates.

Hillocks, G., Jr. (1986). *Research on written composition: New directions for teaching.* Urbana, IL: National Council of Teachers of English.

Johnson, D. W., & Johnson, R. T. (1990). Cooperative learning and achievement. In S. Sharan (Ed.), *Cooperative Learning: Theory and Research* (pp. 23–37). New York: Praeger.

Johnson, D. W., Murayama, G., Johnson, R. T., Nelson, D., & Skon, L. C. (1981). Effects of cooperative, competitive, and individualistic goal structures on achievement: A meta-analysis. *Psychological Bulletin, 89*(1), 47–62.

Johnson, J., Arumi, A. M., & Ott, A. (2006). How Black and Hispanic families rate their schools. *Reality Check 2006.* Accessed at https://files.eric.ed.gov /fulltext/ED493659.pdf on May 10, 2022.

Jones, S. M., & Kahn, J. (2017, September). *The evidence base for how we learn: Supporting students' social, emotional, and academic development.* Accessed at www.aspeninstitute.org/wp-content/uploads/2018/03/FINAL _CDS-Evidence-Base.pdf on August 2, 2022.

King, A. (2002). Structuring peer interaction to promote high-level cognitive processing. *Theory Into Practice, 41*(1), 33–39. http://dx.doi.org/10.1207 /s15430421tip4101_6

Knight, J. (2021, November 1). *The learning zone: The conversation workout* [Blog post]. Accessed at www.ascd.org/el/articles/the-learning-zone-the -conversation-workout on November 21, 2021.

Kriete, R., & Davis, C. (2014). *The morning meeting book: K–8* (3rd ed.). Turners Falls, MA: Northeast Foundation for Children, Inc.

Langreo, L. (2022). *How much time should schools spend on social emotional learning?* Accessed at https://rb.gy/3ipgpy on May 24, 2022.

Leithwood, K. (2006). *Teacher working conditions that matter: Evidence for change.* Toronto, Ontario, Canada: Elementary Teachers Federation of Ontario. Accessed at www.academia.edu/29343982/Teacher_Working_Conditions _That_Matter_Evidence_for_Change on May 12, 2022.

Lomba, A. (2012, June 22). *The "silent period" in language acquisition: Truth or myth?* [Blog post]. Accessed at www.analomba.com/anas-blog/the-silent -period-in-language-acquisition-truth-or-myth/ on May 30, 2022.

Lubbers, M. J., Van Der Werf, M. P. C., Snijders, T. A. B., Creemers, B. P. M., & Kuyper, H. (2006). The impact of peer relations on academic progress in junior high. *Journal of School Psychology, 44*(6), 491–512.

Merrow, C. (n.d.). *Journaling as a social emotional learning practice* [Blog post]. Accessed at empoweringeducation.org/blog/journaling-as-a-social -emotional-practice/ on May 25, 2022.

Mielke, C. (2021, November 1). *The critical element of self-efficacy.* Accessed at www.ascd.org/el/articles/the-critical-element-of-self-efficacy on May 12, 2022.

Moats, L. C. (2020). *Teaching reading is rocket science: What expert teachers of reading should know and be able to do.* Accessed at www.aft.org/ae /summer2020/moats on March 17, 2022.

Nagy, W. (2005). Why vocabulary instruction needs to be long-term and comprehensive. In E. H. Hiebert & M. L. Kamil (Eds.), *Teaching and learning vocabulary: Bringing research to practice* (pp. 27–44). Mahwah, NJ: Lawrence Erlbaum Associates.

The Nation's Report Card. (n.d.). *NAEP long-term trend assessment results: Reading and mathematics.* Accessed at www.nationsreportcard.gov/ltt/?age=9 on August 2, 2022.

Najarro, I. (2021, November 3). *The complicated picture of English-language learners' progress during the pandemic.* Accessed at www.edweek.org/teaching -learning/the-complicated-picture-of-english-language-learners-progress -during-the-pandemic/2021/11 on August 2, 2022.

National Aeronautics and Space Administration Goddard Institute for Space Studies. (2010, January 2). *2009: Second warmest year on record; end of warmest decade.* Accessed at https://climate.nasa.gov/news/249/2009 -second-warmest-year-on-record-end-of-warmest-decade on May 25, 2022.

National Academies of Sciences, Engineering, and Medicine. (2017). *Promoting the educational success of children and youth learning English: Promising futures.* Washington, DC: National Academies Press.

National Council of Teachers of English. (2008). *English language learners.* Accessed at https://cdn.ncte.org/nctefiles/resources/policyresearch /ellresearchbrief.pdf on May 25, 2022.

National Equity Project. (n.d.). *Social emotional learning and equity.* Accessed at www.nationalequityproject.org/frameworks/social-emotional-learning -and-equity on August 4, 2022.

National Reading Panel. (2000). *Teaching children to read: An evidence-based assessment of the scientific research literature on reading and its implications for reading instruction.* Rockville, MD: National Institute of Child Health and Human Development.

Olsen, L. (2010). *Reparable harm: Fulfilling the unkept promise of educational opportunity for California's long term English learners.* Accessed at www .shastacoe.org/uploaded/Dept/is/LCAP-Local_Control_Accountability _Plans/ReparableHarm2ndedition.pdf on August 5, 2022.

Panchal, N., Kamal, R., Cox, C., Garfield, R., & Chidambaram, P. (2021, May 26). *Mental health and substance use considerations among children during the COVID-19 pandemic.* Accessed at www.kff.org/coronavirus-covid-19 /issue-brief/mental-health-and-substance-use-considerations-among -children-during-the-covid-19-pandemic on March 17, 2022.

Patrick, K., Socol, A., Grossman, J., & Shih, M. B. (2021). *Strategies to solve unfinished learning*. Accessed at https://edtrust.org/strategies-to-solve-unfinished-learning/ on June 4, 2022.

Pearson, P. D., Moje, E., & Greenleaf, C. (2010, April 23). Literacy and science: Each in the service of the other. *NIH Science, 328*(5977), 459–463.

PsychPage. (n.d.). *List of feeling words*. Accessed at www.psychpage.com/learning/library/assess/feelings.html on August 8, 2022.

Regional Educational Laboratory West. (2016, November). Long-term English learner students: Spotlight on an overlooked population. Accessed at www.wested.org/wp-content/uploads/2016/11/LTEL-factsheet.pdf on August 2, 2022.

Rogers, L. A., & Graham, S. (2008). A meta-analysis of single subject design writing intervention research. *Journal of Educational Psychology, 100*(4). 879–906.

Roseth, C. J., Johnson, D. W., & Johnson, R. T. (2008). Promoting early adolescents' achievement and peer relationships: The effects of cooperative, competitive, and individualistic goal structures. *Psychological Bulletin, 134*(2), 223–246.

Sahakyan, N., & Cook, H. G. (2021). *Examining English learner testing, proficiency, and growth: Before and throughout the COVID-19 pandemic*. Madison, WI: Wisconsin Center for Education Research. Accessed at https://wida.wisc.edu/sites/default/files/resource/Report-Examining-English-Learner-Testing-Proficiency-Growth.pdf on May 9, 2022.

Santiago-Poventud, L., Corbett, N. J., Daunic, A. P., Aydin, B., Lane, H., & Smith, S. W. (2015). Developing social-emotional vocabulary to support self-regulation for young children at risk for emotional and behavioral problems. *International Journal of School and Cognitive Psychology, 2*(143).

Schmoker, M. (2021, May 1). The obvious path to better professional development. *Educational Leadership, 78*(8), 65–69.

Sedova, K., Sedláček, M., Švaříček, R., Majcík, M., Navrátilová, J., Drexlerova, A., et al. (2019). Do those who talk more learn more? The relationship between student classroom talk and student achievement. *Learning and Instruction, 63*(1).

Sénéchal, M., & Cornell, E. H. (1993). Vocabulary acquisition through shared reading experiences. *Reading Research Quarterly*, *28*(4), 360–374.

Shachar, H., & Sharan, S. (1994). Talking, relating, and achieving: Effects of cooperative learning and whole-class instruction. *Cognition and Instruction*, *12*(4), 313–353.

Shanahan, T. (2002, November). *A sin of the second kind: The neglect of fluency instruction and what we can do about it* [Slideware presentation]. Accessed at https://shanahanonliteracy.com/upload/publications/26/pdf/teaching -fluency-instructon.ppt on August 3, 2022.

Short, D. J., & Fitzsimmons, S. (2007). *Double the work: Challenges and solutions to acquiring language and academic literacy for adolescent English language learners.* Washington, DC: Alliance for Excellent Education.

Slavin, R. E. (1989). Cooperative learning and student achievement. In R. E. Slavin (Ed.), *School and classroom organization* (pp. 129–156). Mahwah, NJ: Lawrence Erlbaum Associates.

Slavin, R. E. (2014). Cooperative learning and academic achievement: Why does groupwork work? *Anales de Psicología*, *30*(3), 785–791.

Slavin, R. E., & Calderón, M. E. (Eds.). (2001). *Effective programs for Latino students.* Mahwah, NJ: Lawrence Erlbaum Associates.

Slavin, R. E., Madden, N., Calderón, M. E., Chamberlain, A., & Hennessy M. (2009). *Fifth-year reading and language outcomes of a randomized evaluation of transitional bilingual education: Report to IES.* Washington, DC: Institute for Education Sciences, U.S. Department of Education.

Snow, C. E., Griffin, P., & Burns, M. S. (Eds.). (2005). *Knowledge to support the teaching of reading: Preparing teachers for a changing world.* San Francisco: Jossey-Bass.

Sparks, S. D. (2021, June 15). *Is the bottom falling out for readers who struggle the most?* Accessed at www.edweek.org/teaching-learning/is-the-bottom -falling-out-for-readers-who-struggle-the-most/2021/06 on August 8, 2022.

Stahl, S. A. (2005). Four problems with teaching word meanings: And what to do to make vocabulary and integral part of instruction. In E. H. Hiebert & M. L. Kamil (Eds.), *Teaching and learning vocabulary: Bringing research to practice* (pp. 95–114). Mahwah, NJ: Lawrence Erlbaum Associates.

Stevens, R. J. (2003). Student team reading and writing: A cooperative learning approach to middle school literacy instruction. *Educational Research and Evaluation, 9*(2). 137–160.

Téllez, K., & Waxman, H. C. (Eds.). (2006). *Preparing quality educators for English language learners: Research, policy, and practice.* Mahwah, NJ: Lawrence Erlbaum Associates.

Tharp, R. G., Estrada, P., Dalton, S. S., & Yamauchi, L. A. (2000). *Teaching transformed: Achieving excellence, fairness, inclusion, and harmony.* Boulder, CO: Westview Press.

Wang, M. C., Haertel, G. D., & Walberg, H. J. (1997). Fostering educational resilience in inner-city schools. In H. J. Walberg, O. Reyes, & R. P. Weissberg (Eds.), *Children and youth: Interdisciplinary perspectives* (pp. 119–140). Thousand Oaks, CA: SAGE.

What Works Clearinghouse. (n.d.). *Quick reference resources about WWC processes.* Accessed at https://ies.ed.gov/ncee/wwc/WhatWeDo on May 24, 2022.

What Works Clearinghouse. (2007). *ESL in the content areas.* Accessed at https://ies.ed.gov/ncee/wwc/EvidenceSnapshot/163 on August 3, 2022.

What Works Clearinghouse. (2013, February). *Sheltered Instruction Observation Protocol (SIOP).* Accessed at https://ies.ed.gov/ncee/wwc/Docs /InterventionReports/wwc_siop_022013.pdf on August 4, 2022.

Yale Center for Emotional Intelligence. (2022). *What is RULER?* Accessed at https://www.rulerapproach.org/about/what-is-ruler/ on August 4, 2022.

Zacarian, D., Calderón, M. E., & Gottlieb, M. (2021). *Beyond crises: Overcoming linguistic and cultural inequities in communities, schools, and classrooms.* Thousand Oaks, CA: Corwin.

Zins, J. E., Weissberg, R. P., Wang, M. C., & Walberg, H. J. (Eds.). (2004). *Building academic success on social and emotional learning: What does the research say?* New York: Teachers College Press.

Index

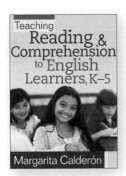

Teaching Reading and Comprehension to English Learners, K–5
Margarita Espino Calderón

Raise achievement for English learners through new instructional strategies and assessment processes. This book addresses the language, literacy, and content instructional needs of ELs and frames quality instruction within effective schooling structures and the implementation of response to intervention.

BKF402

Literacy Strategies for English Learners in Core Content Secondary Classrooms
Margarita Espino Calderón, Maria N. Trejo, and Hector Montenegro With Argelia Carreón, Timothy D'Emilio, Joanne Marino, and Joy Kreeft Peyton

Motivate English learners to boost proficiency with confidence. Working within the framework of the Common Core and other state standards, this book focuses on instructional strategies that integrate language, literacy, and content across subject areas to ensure *all* students thrive.

BKF615

Promises Fulfilled
Margarita Espino Calderón and Shawn Slakk With Hector Montenegro

Discover research-based strategies preK–12 administrators and teacher leaders can implement to effectively identify and support English learners. Each chapter ends with discussion questions readers should share with staff or team members to promote EL success schoolwide.

BKF774

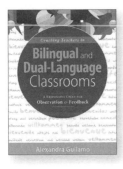

Coaching Teachers in Bilingual and Dual-Language Classrooms
Alexandra Guilamo

Gain the skills you need to coach teachers in bilingual and dual-language classrooms. In this practical guide, you will discover a proven process for creating a fair and effective observation and feedback cycle to help support teachers in this important work.

BKF918

Solution Tree | Press
a division of
Solution Tree

Visit SolutionTree.com or call 800.733.6786 to order.

Wait! **Your professional development journey doesn't have to end with the last pages of this book.**

We realize improving student learning doesn't happen overnight. And your school or district shouldn't be left to puzzle out all the details of this process alone.

No matter where you are on the journey, we're committed to helping you get to the next stage.

Take advantage of everything from **custom workshops** to **keynote presentations** and **interactive web and video conferencing**. We can even help you develop an action plan tailored to fit your specific needs.

Let's get the conversation started.

Call 888.763.9045 today.

SolutionTree.com